The
Moon
Gardener's
Almanac
2019

Created by Céleste
Edited by Thérèse Trédoulat
Translated by Mado Spiegler and Polly Lawson

First published in French as *Jardinez avec la Lune 2019*
by Éditions Rustica in 2018
This edition published in English by Floris Books in 2018
© 2018 Éditions Rustica, Paris
English version © 2018 Floris Books

British Library CIP data available
ISBN 978-1 78250-518-1
Printed & bound by MBM Print SCS Ltd, Glasgow

The
Moon
Gardener's
Almanac
2019

Floris
Books

Contents

Foreword

This almanac will help you to grow vegetables, fruit, flowers, shrubs and trees successfully from January 1 to December 31 using the lunar cycle as your guide. Based on 35 years' experience of gardening with the Moon, we explain how, by following the ascending or descending movements of the Moon and the constellations it crosses, you can optimise plant growth, leading to more abundant harvests and crops rich in vitamins and flavour.

Day by day, the calendar suggests favourable times for working with different types of plant – leaf, flower, fruit or root – as well as highlighting less favourable times: apogees, perigees, lunar nodes and eclipses. Key gardening tasks and methods are described throughout the year, such as when and where to sow cauliflowers and tomatoes, how to prune and graft fruit trees, and when to seed your lawn.

There are informative sections on how to garden naturally by avoiding chemical treatments, respecting the soil, and employing natural practices such as crop rotation and companion planting, all of which will make your garden more resilient and your crops healthier.

Monthly charts allow you to make notes about the weather, temperature and air pressure, which all have a huge influence on our gardens. By comparing several years in a row, you can follow the evolution of the climate and adapt your gardening methods accordingly. If the calendar dates don't suit your climate, the crop tables offer alternative favourable dates for sowing, planting, thinning, harvesting and pruning according to the Moon.

We wish you happy reading and fruitful gardening throughout the year!

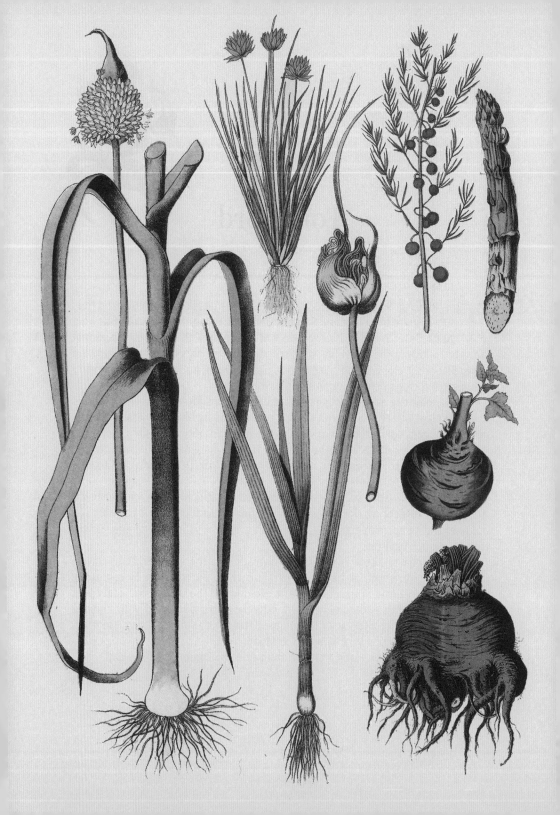

The Moon
and the
Garden

Rhythms
of the Earth

The life rhythms of our Earth involve three recurring processes: the annual cycle ruled by the Sun; the monthly cycle ruled by the Moon; and the daily cycle, ruled by the alternation of day and night.

Annual cycle

To help us understand the path of the Moon and its effects, which are the foundation of our gardening calendar, let's first look at the path of the Sun in the temperate zone of the Northern hemisphere.

Winter and spring

On the winter solstice, December 21 (the shortest day of the year, varying in the UK from 8 hours 3 minutes in Penzance, Cornwall, to only 5 hours 49 minutes in Lerwick, Shetland), the Sun rises well to the south-east and makes its lowest arc of the year, setting far in the south-west. By this time, many plants have died or are lying dormant in the soil. The Earth begins to prepare for its renewal – the new solar year is starting.

From the shortest day onwards to the summer solstice on June 21 (the longest day of the year, varying from 16 hours 23 minutes in Penzance to 18 hours 55 minutes in Lerwick), the Sun rises higher and higher in the sky. It ascends from Sagittarius, the lowest constellation, to Taurus and Gemini, the highest constellations. During these six months, very gradually, the Earth warms up. As the midday Sun gets higher in the sky and the days get longer, sap becomes active in the plant world.

It is then that we witness a veritable resurrection of nature, which guides the gardener's many tasks: pruning fruit and ornamental trees, soil preparation, sowing and replanting. In June, this time of intense growth comes to an end, as does summer sowing – harvesting is about to start.

Summer and autumn

On June 21, the day of the summer solstice, the Sun starts its descending arc. Its warm rays now have a drying effect. The days grow shorter, crops are harvested and the Earth starts to become bare. The rise of sap also slows down, causing tree leaves to dry out.

After the autumn equinox on September 22, gardeners can gradually start to work the soil in preparation for the following year.

With every harvest, the soil becomes less fertile, its vital resources exhausted by the crops, vegetables and fruit it has nourished. We need to help it restore itself by providing refined compost, enlivening manures and invigorating green manures.

During this period of deep inhalation, the Earth absorbs all the fertilising and rebalancing elements that gardeners provide. Sap descends into the roots again, leaves blow away, days get shorter and shorter and winter arrives. At the lowest point of the cycle, with the Sun back in Sagittarius, a new exhalation is about to begin.

Now, on warm, calm days, is the time for gardeners to plant perennials, trees and bare-root bushes.

Position of the Earth in relation to the constellations of the zodiac

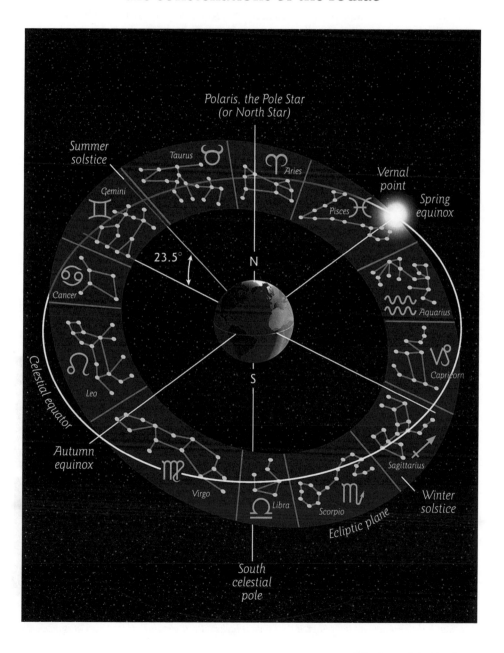

Monthly cycle

The Moon takes one lunar month to orbit the Earth (approximately 27 days). Just as the Sun does in one year, in one month the Moon passes in front of every zodiacal constellation, with profound effects upon the Earth. The most spectacular example of this is illustrated by the phenomenon of the tides, which follow the rhythm of the 'Moon Day' of 24 hours and 50 minutes, of the Moon's rising, culminating, setting, reaching its lowest point and rising again. Scientific experiments have shown that the effect of the Moon can even be measured on inland water bodies.

Try looking up at the sky every evening. Whenever you can see the Moon, select landmarks (perhaps a tree, a house, or a hill) to locate it in relation to your environment. Day after day, you will observe the Moon ascending or descending in relation to these landmarks.

A number of online and print resources will give you daily times of the moonrise and moonset, which, on average, are about 50 minutes later every day.

Ascending moon: the lunar 'spring'

For 13½ days, the Moon ascends from Sagittarius, the lowest constellation, to Taurus/Gemini, the highest. It follows the path taken by the Sun from December 21 to June 21. During this time, sap rises in all plant life, swelling their aerial parts. Now is the time to remove grafts for later use (making sure to keep them at the right temperature until it's time to graft them). It is also time for sowing seeds, harvesting leafy vegetables, juicy fruit, and cutting flowers for bouquets.

Descending moon: the lunar 'autumn'

For the next 13½ days, as the Moon descends from Taurus to Sagittarius, it will appear lower and lower on the horizon every day. It follows the path taken by the Sun from June 21 to December 21. The sap goes back down into the roots and, as in October, the earth is at its most absorbent.

Using a tree as a landmark, look at the Moon and make a note of the time.
Look at it the next day, an hour later. If the Moon is higher, it is ascending; if it is lower, it is descending.

Now is the time to plant, replant, spread compost and organic manures, and prune. Plants recover better during this time: the roots reach deeper; the earth assimilates fertilizers well; hedges tolerate pruning without any problem, and the wounds left by removing tree branches heal better.

We call the ascending and descending movement of the Moon in a month (to be precise, 27 days, 7 hours, 43 minutes and 11 seconds) the sidereal period. **It is this ascending and descending motion that is relevant in the garden.**

Waxing and waning moon

Another cycle, called the synodic period (or synodic month) also takes approximately one month (to be precise, 29 days, 12 hours, 44 minutes and 3 seconds). **We do not take this cycle into account when gardening with the Moon.**

During the synodic month, the Moon waxes from New Moon to Full Moon, with the nearest side becoming increasingly visible. A thin sickle appears, which grows larger every day, to become the First Quarter and eventually the Full Moon.

The Moon then wanes to a New Moon. At the time of the Full Moon, it is fully illuminated by the Sun and looks completely round, waning daily until it disappears again at the time of the New Moon.

NOTE: Do not confuse the ascending moon with the waxing moon, or the descending moon with the waning moon.

Daily cycle

If you have ever camped in the woods, you will have been woken by a marvellous chorus of birdsong an hour or two before sunrise. The air grows colder, humidity rises, and plants also awaken, opening up to the morning dew and starting to swell with sap.

In the morning, when the dew has disappeared, it's time to sow seeds and pick lettuce, spinach, cucumbers and anything else that grows above ground.

Later, between midday and 3 pm, as the Sun starts to descend, the Earth turns back inward and forces move towards plants' roots. Now is the time to plant, replant, harvest root vegetables and finally, after sundown, to water.

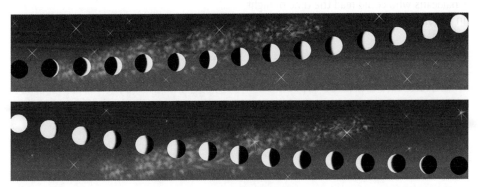

Top: The New Moon, invisible in the sky, waxes through crescent, First Quarter (half Moon), gibbous to Full Moon, getting bigger every day, until it appears as a full circle.

Bottom: The round Full Moon wanes through gibbous, Last Quarter (half Moon), crescent, and ends with the New Moon.

Tradition and the Moon

The Moon, being an ever-changing heavenly body, has always intrigued humans. We have long looked for connections between its phases and weather forecasts, health, births, animals and plants. For example, mushrooms can rarely be found at the time of the New Moon, even if the season and moisture are favourable, as this is their gestating period. They begin to appear on the fifth day of the lunar phase cycle and will be magnificently tender and succulent at the time of the Full Moon, or a little earlier. As the Moon wanes, their growth slows down and they gradually dry out.

Constellations of the Zodiac

Going back to prehistory, humans studied the stars. The first records come from the Chaldeans who could read the time of night in the sky, orient themselves and follow the seasons.

Lunar months or periods

There are four major lunar periods, each about a month in length.

Sidereal period

As we saw above, the sidereal period is the time it takes for the Moon to return to the same star in its revolution around the Earth. It is 27 days, 7 hours, 43 minutes and 12 seconds.

Synodic period

The synodic period refers to the phases of the Moon. As early as the third century BC, Babylonians had precisely calculated the average duration between two similar lunar phases (for example, two Full Moons) to an accuracy of 5 seconds. The average duration of the synodic period is 29 days, 12 hours, 44 minutes and 3 seconds.

Anomalistic (or apsidal) period

In its elliptical orbit the Moon is sometimes further from the Earth (apogee) and sometimes closer (perigee). The time from one perigee (or apogee) to the next is 27 days, 13 hours, 18 minutes and 33 seconds on average.

Draconitic (or nodal) revolution

The Moon's path through the stars does not exactly follow the Sun's path (the ecliptic). Its orbit is inclined by about 5 degrees to the ecliptic, crossing it twice at 'nodes'. The ascending node is where the Moon crosses from south of the ecliptic to north. The descending node is where it crosses from north of the ecliptic to south. The time between successive passages of the Moon through the same nodes is 27 days, 5 hours, 5 minutes and 36 seconds.

The twelve constellations

The 'fixed stars' have a constant relationship to each other even though they move across the sky, some rising and setting. Since ancient times these fixed stars have been seen in groups or constellations. The Sun, the Moon and the planets continually travel through a band of these fixed stars. This band consists of twelve constellations, which were seen as twelve animals or living beings in ancient Mesopotamia and Egypt. Hence the name *zodiac* (Greek *zoon*: animal, living being). You will always be able to pick out these constellations along the path followed by the Moon from the billions of stars surrounding us. The zodiac is a wide band of 18° around the line of the ecliptic, or ecliptic plane. Each star is a sun like ours. Some are much bigger than our Sun (Aldebaran, the most brilliant star in Taurus, has a diameter 36 times that of the Sun). Each of these stars, like our Sun, sends us its distant rays and we benefit from the influences of the constellation and its sky region. Let's take a look at these possible influences.

The precession of the equinoxes

Between March 20 and 22, depending on the year, the Sun crosses the celestial equator at the *vernal point*, marking the beginning of spring. This very specific point does not stay fixed in relation to the stars. It moves back every year by a 50 seconds of arc which comes to 1° over 72 years, or 30° over 2,160 years. This means that the vernal point which in Greek times was in the constellation of Aries, has now moved to the constellation of Pisces.

The Greeks divided the zodiac into twelve equal *signs* of 30° each. These *signs* are still used in astrology today. However for this calendar it is the visible *constellations* which are used. Because of the precession of the equinox the signs and constellations have shifted on average by one constellation.

The four elements

Just as a plant is composed of four parts – root, leaf, flower and fruit – the twelve zodiacal regions each have affinities with one of the main elements of the universe – earth, water, air and fire. These form four types of impulse regularly distributed around the Earth, and each impulse has a specific effect on particular parts of plants.

When it passes in front of a constellation, the Moon activates these different forces. It captures them, adds its own power then reflects them back to Earth just as it reflects the light of the Sun. Whenever gardeners work the soil, they make it more receptive to the influence of these elements.

The earth element

Attuned to the constellations of **Taurus, Virgo and Capricorn**, the earth element affects the buried part of the plant: the root. When the Moon passes in front of these earth constellations, it's the optimum time to enrich and prepare the soil, plant seeds, thin, weed, and transplant the seedlings of root vegetables. In particular, these constellations influence root and bulb crops such as garlic, onions, carrots, turnips, potatoes and radishes. When we respect this timing, these vegetables are more resistant to parasites

Constellations of the zodiac

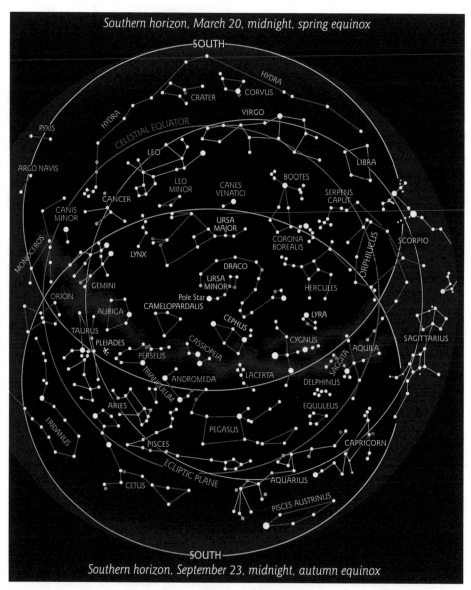

Southern horizon, March 20, midnight, spring equinox

SOUTH

SAGITTARIUS

SCORPIO

LIBRA

HYDRA

CRATER

CORVUS

VIRGO

CELESTIAL EQUATOR

PYXIS

ARGO NAVIS

LEO

LEO MINOR

CANES VENATICI

BOOTES

SERPENS CAPUT

CANCER

CANIS MINOR

URSA MAJOR

CORONA BOREALIS

ORPHIUEUS

MONOCEROS

LYNX

DRACO

HERCULES

URSA MINOR

GEMINI

ORION

Pole Star

CAMELOPARDALIS

CEPHUS

LYRA

AURIGA

TAURUS

PLEIADES

CASSIOPEIA

CYGNUS

AQUILA

SAGITTA

PERSEUS

ANDROMEDA

LACERTA

DELPHINUS

TRIANGULUM

ARIES

EQUULEUS

ERIDANUS

PISCES

PEGASUS

CAPRICORN

CETUS

ECLIPTIC PLANE

AQUARIUS

PISCES AUSTRINUS

SOUTH

Southern horizon, September 23, midnight, autumn equinox

The top circular area of the illustration represents the sky at midnight on March 20, day of the spring equinox; the lower circular area, the sky at midnight on September 23, day of the autumn equinox. The constellations of the zodiac are along the ecliptic, the path followed every year by the Sun, and every month by the Moon.

when harvested, and their nutritional value, taste and productivity increase.

The water element

Active in **Cancer, Scorpio and Pisces**, the water element particularly influences moisture-loving parts of the plant: the stem and leaves.

Gardeners should use times when the Moon passes in front of water constellations to care for leaf and stem crops such as lettuce, spinach and asparagus. Doing so will yield beautiful, tender, crunchy leaves and delicate, tasty asparagus.

The air element

Due to its affinity with **Gemini, Libra and Aquarius**, the air element expresses itself in the fragrance of flowers, plants and vegetables. For optimum results, gardeners should use times when the Moon passes in front of air constellations to take care of flowers and flower crops such as artichokes, cauliflowers and broccoli.

The fire element

Related to **Aries, Leo and Sagittarius**, the fire element brings the warmth needed to ripen fruit and the seeds necessary for reproduction. Gardeners should use times when the Moon is in fire constellations to care for fruit and seed crops such as apricots, apples, peas, tomatoes and beans.

When gardening by element, be aware that some constellations are isolated, e.g. Gemini and Cancer, while others almost overlap, e.g. Taurus and Aries.

NOTE: The calendar gives very precise timings for the transition between ascending and descending moons (or vice versa), as well as for the passage between constellations. Gardeners should not rush to work as soon as it is 'the right time', for the effect is not instantaneous. Instead take time to think and plan the garden long-term. Also, remember that schedules are given for Greenwich Mean Time, so if you are not in Britain or Ireland you will need to make adjustments for local times (see p. 37).

Variable durations

The zodiac constellations are different lengths, which results in unequal time periods for gardening certain types of plant. In practice, this means that gardeners will always have more time for root vegetables than for flowers.
Earth constellations occupy:
Capricorn 28° + Taurus 36° + Virgo 46° = 110°
Water constellations: Pisces 38° + Cancer 21° + Scorpio 31° = 90°
Fire constellations: Sagittarius 30° + Aries 24° + Leo 35° = 89°
Air constellations: Aquarius 25° + Gemini 28° + Libra 18° = 71°

What if I can't always follow the Moon faithfully?

It's not always possible to strictly follow the Moon; it might be too cold, or just impossible to make time to garden. You can compensate by making sure you perform as many pre-harvest tasks at the most favourable time. If possible, prioritise the preparation and enrichment of soil, sowing and planting.

Current position of the zodiac constellations
and corresponding symbols in Western astrology

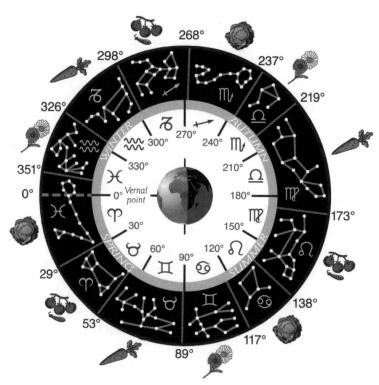

The inner circle shows the twelve signs of the zodiac as shown in horoscopes. In astrology, their size is a constant (30° each). The outer circle shows the constellations as they should be observed in gardening: for instance, the smallest constellation, Libra, covers 237°– 219° = 18°, not 30° as in astrology. **When you garden, make sure you follow the actual duration of each constellation as our calendar does.**

Zodiac constellations	♈ Aries	♌ Leo	♐ Sagittarius
	♉ Taurus	♍ Virgo	♑ Capricorn
	♊ Gemini	♎ Libra	♒ Aquarius
	♋ Cancer	♏ Scorpio	♓ Pisces

Explanation of gardening symbols

LEAF
Water constellations

FLOWER
Air constellations

ROOT
Earth constellations

SEED & FRUIT
Fire constellations

Lunar Irregularities

There are times when the Moon does not provide the optimum conditions for gardening, specifically during periods of significant lunar change. Be sure to wait 5 hours either side of a moon node, apogee or perigee before gardening and, if possible, wait even longer if there is an eclipse.

Perigee and apogee

The Moon travels on an elliptical orbit, in which the centre of Earth is one of the foci. Every lunar month, the Moon passes through the **perigee**, the point where its distance from the Earth is smallest (356,500 km/221,500 miles) and its speed greatest (moving 15° per day). Conversely, at the **apogee**, the Moon is at its most distant point (406,700 km /252,700 miles) and its speed is at its slowest (moving 12° per day). Gardening during the Moon's perigee can result in weak and sickly plants, while vegetation can be shrunken, constricted and prone to sickness when planted during the apogee.

If the Full Moon or the New Moon coincide with the perigee, there is an even greater likelihood of irregularities, particularly if it coincides with an equinox or solstice. This was the case during Storm Martin, which violently swept across Europe in December 1999. Likewise, the devastating tsunami of December 2004 took place at the time of the winter solstice, on the eve of the Moon's apogee on December 27.

To avoid a weak harvest, watch out for these situations: Sun at the time of equinox or solstice + Full Moon, and New Moon at the perigee.

Moon nodes

The plane of the Moon's orbit is at an angle of 5.1° from the plane of the ecliptic, along which the Sun travels. The Moon crosses this plane twice every month, at two points called nodes. (The ascending node is when the Moon crosses from south of the ecliptic to north. The descending node is where it crosses from north of the ecliptic to south.) When the Full Moon or New Moon coincides with a node, there is an eclipse of the Moon or the Sun. Plants are particularly sensitive at these times, so keep in mind that sowing will produce sterile seeds. You may also often notice that the sky is white during a moon node. Again, it is best not to garden 5 hours before or after this point.

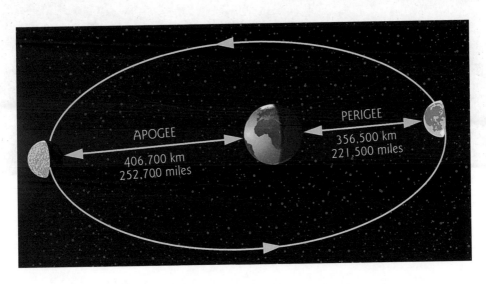

APOGEE
406,700 km
252,700 miles

PERIGEE
356,500 km
221,500 miles

The Moon after Easter

While the true power of the Moon is constantly being discussed and argued, in agriculture the influence of the Moon after Easter has always been unquestioned. The most ancient texts bear witness to it, and gardeners still watch out for its coming.

Easter always occurs after the Full Moon after the spring equinox. At this time of year, the Sun is already high and the days last longer. When the sky is clear, daytime temperatures begin to rise, allowing small seedlings and budding fruit to soak up the warmth. After sunset, the cold returns and the thermometer dips; gradually a cold dew covers the plants and it can sometimes still be frosty at dawn. Young plants can often suffer during these cold nights, so keep any weather protection in place during this time.

Eclipses

If the New Moon occurs near a node (see p. 19) there is a solar eclipse. If the Full Moon coincides with a node, there will be a lunar eclipse. Plants are extremely sensitive to these phenomena, so it is advisable to avoid gardening during these times.

Moon nodes

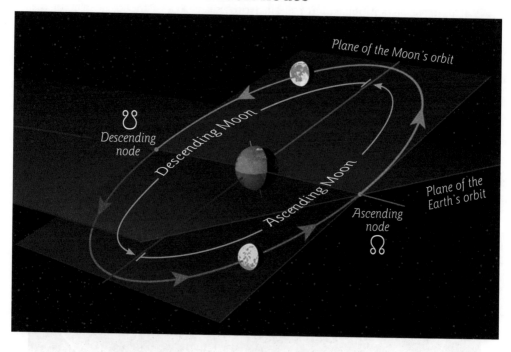

The Moon and Plants

Every type of plant is affected differently by the Moon's position in each constellation. Vegetables can be classified as root, leaf, flower or fruit depending on the plant part we consume. For example, beetroot, onion and potatoes are all roots; chard, cabbage and Brussels sprouts are leaves; artichokes and broccoli are flowers; and tomatoes, aubergine (or eggplant) and peas are fruit, as are grains and fruit trees.

Root, leaf, flower or fruit?

Below is a partial list of vegetables, ornamental plants and fruit trees.
Adapt the list to match what you plan to cultivate.

Root	Leaf	Flower	Seed and Fruit
Beet(root)	Asparagus	Broccoli	Aubergine (eggplant)
Carrot	Brussels sprout	Cauliflower	Berries
Celeriac	Cabbage	Globe artichoke	Broad bean (fava)
Chervil (root)	Cardoon		Chilli pepper
Chicory*	Celery	Flowering bushes	Courgette (zucchini)
Chinese artichoke	Chicory*	– Forsythia	Cucumber
Garlic	Cress	– Lilac	Fruit trees
Horseradish	Dandelion	– Magnolia	Green bean
Jerusalem artichoke	Endive*	– Rose	Lentils
Leek	Fennel	– Wisteria	Marrow
Onion	Grass		Melon
Parsnip	Herbs	Flowers	Peas
Potato	Lettuce	– Annuals	Pepper
Radish	Lamb's lettuce	– Biennials	Pumpkin
Salsify	(mâche)	– Bulbs	Strawberry
Shallot	Ornamental bushes	– Perennials	Squash
Swede (rutabaga)	Purslane		Tomato
Turnip	Rhubarb		Watermelon
	Rocket (arugula)		
	Romaine lettuce		Grains
	Sorrel		– Barley
	Spinach		– Corn
	Swiss chard		– Oats
			– Rye
			– Wheat

NOTE: *The cultivation of endive and chicory has two stages. The aim with the original seeding is to produce strong roots, so sow the seed in an ascending moon, on a root day. Pull them up, again on a root day, and let them dry a few days on the ground. The second stage – forcing – aims to produce beautiful leaves, ideal for cooking or salads. This is achieved by replanting the roots and harvesting the leaves on leaf days.*

Gardening According to the Moon's Position

In order to benefit from the influence of the Moon, particular types of plants should be sown according to whether the Moon is ascending or descending, and which constellation it is passing through. For example, by looking at the grid below we can see that lettuce (a leaf crop) is best sown in an ascending moon when the Moon is in Pisces, and that forsythia (a flower) should be planted in a descending moon when the Moon passes in front of Gemini or Libra.

Movement of the Moon	Constellation/element	Type of plant	Task
Ascending	Sagittarius ♐ Fire 30°	Seed and fruit	In the ascending Moon:
Ascending	Capricorn ♑ Earth 28°	Root	• Sow • Harvest leaf crops (spinach, lettuce) • Harvest flower crops (artichokes) • Harvest fruit (tomatoes, peas, apples) • Take cuttings and graft
Ascending	Aquarius ♒ Air 25°	Flower	
Ascending	Pisces ♓ Water 38°	Leaf	
Ascending	Aries ♈ Fire 24°	Seed and fruit	
Ascending	Taurus ♉ Earth 36°	Root	
Ascending	Gemini ♊ Air 28°	Flower	

Movement of the Moon	Constellation/ element	Type of plant	Task
Descending	Gemini ♊ Air 28°	Flower	In the descending Moon:
Descending	Cancer ♋ Water 21°	Leaf	• Propagate from cuttings
Descending	Leo ♌ Fire 35°	Seed and fruit	• Enrich the soil • Thin seedlings • Transplant seedlings
Descending	Virgo ♍ Earth 46°	Root	• Harvest root crops (carrots, turnips)
Descending	Libra ♎ Air 18°	Flower	• Prune and cut back
Descending	Scorpio ♏ Water 31°	Leaf	• Divide plants • Layer
Descending	Sagittarius ♐ Fire 30°	Seed and fruit	

The descending Moon ends in Gemini and the ascending Moon starts in Sagittarius. Following our calendar allows you to match your garden activities with the movement of the Moon in the sky.

Plants in their Environment

As a living being fixed in the soil, a plant is entirely dependent on its environment. On one hand, it raises its stem towards the sky to catch the light and warmth of the Sun, while on the other, it plunges its roots into the Earth looking for everything it needs to grow and reproduce. Food, water, minerals and cosmic life forces are all essential to a plant's survival, and the condition of the soil is vitally important in ensuring these resources are successfully delivered.

Cosmic forces

We can aid plants' sensitivity to cosmic influences by doing all we can to increase their receptiveness. Suppressing artificial obstacles to cosmic forces, making the atmosphere permeable, and introducing easily assimilated food into the soil all help to optimise plants' sensitivity. By making the helpful cosmic forces as accessible as possible, we will see the benefit in the roots, leaves, flowers and fragrances of our gardens.

Most cosmic forces, in particular those of the Moon, act only indirectly on plants; before roots can take them in, they are absorbed by the soil – depending on its receptivity and the current position in the lunar cycle. The health and vigour of our vegetables call for well-balanced, aerated and receptive soil.

Soil

In order to develop properly, plants need air, light and soil in which to take root and absorb water and nutrients. These elements are more easily available to plants when the soil's fertility has been restored with beneficial manures and enrichments, which are active during the most favourable lunar dates.

Every soil is different; whether sandy, clay or lime, it will need to be loosened regularly and be fertilised with appropriate growth aids and enlivening manures. **Ensure chemical fertilisers are not used:** besides their harmful effect on crops, they make the soil impervious to the influence of cosmic forces. When gardening with the Moon, feed soil exclusively with well-ripened compost, animal manure, green manures and liquid slurries of vitalising plants, for example nettles and comfrey. Soil should not remain bare between two crops: depending on the season, sow clover, rye, vetch or mustard to contribute helpful organic matter and protect the soil from weathering (see 'Growing green manures' and 'Mulching' p. 26–27).

Air and light

Sunlight is integral to a plant's development. Gardeners should make sure that their growing space has the maximum amount of light, but shouldn't hesitate to plant a hedge of mixed bushes on the side of the prevailing wind for protection. The hedge will filter the air, protecting plants from chemical treatments which might have been applied in neighbouring properties, and will also shelter birds that feed on aphids, caterpillars and unwanted insects.

Improving and feeding the soil

Gardeners who use the Moon can also make the most of their soil by following the general principles of biodynamic gardening (see Further Reading, p. 119). Work the soil without disrupting the direction of the top layer, and improve it with natural matter that will be organically assimilated by the plants on decomposing. Year on year, this will gradually improve the fertility of the soil, enabling the successful growth of healthy vegetables, flowers and fruit.

Working the soil

Soil is alive. It contains millions of micro-organisms invisible to the eye, as well as being home to bigger inhabitants such as earthworms and beetles. On the soil's surface, we find aerobic micro-organisms that need oxygen to survive, while anaerobic organisms live deeper down. Whenever the soil is ploughed, by hand or machine, the top layers are inverted, together with the micro-organisms they contain, which subsequently often die. Yet these minuscule creatures and bacteria are a gardener's allies. They break down organic matter, transforming it into humus, which plants can then use for food and growth.

With this in mind, it is vital that we adopt 'soft' practices for aerating the soil, without disturbing it. Adapted hand cultivators should be used where possible (consisting of two handles connected by a bar at the bottom, in which three to five vertical tines are inserted) and soil should be worked while walking backwards. Plunging the tines into the soil and lowering the handles produces a crumbly, aerated soil, which will in turn create a loose, aerated growing surface.

Making compost

Waste from the garden and kitchen can be turned into excellent compost. Dry or brown garden waste, including bush cuttings (crushed first, if possible) and dead leaves, and green and wet waste from lawn mowing, weeds and vegetable peelings can all be used to create homemade compost. Plants that have gone to seed, sick plants or vegetation affected by parasites (whether eggs, larvae or fully formed) should be avoided, in addition to rose cuttings, fruit-tree leaves and wormy fruit. Waste should be piled up in a corner of the garden or in a composter, alternating dry and wet matter in layers approximately 25 cm (10 in) thick. Ideally, the waste should touch the ground to allow earthworms to rise into the pile and break everything down. You can speed up the process by adding earth worms, which will digest your waste. If necessary, water the pile once a month to hasten the process further, and make sure you cover the pile to keep it warm, which will speed up fermentation. Your compost will be ripe in approximately 10 months. Use it at the end of winter, incorporating it superficially into the soil, spreading it between flowers, in the planting holes of 'greedy' vegetables, fruit trees or berry bushes, and in the mixture you use to repot any potted plants.

Introducing natural fertilisers

More and more garden centres sell 'natural fertilisers' containing the same elements as chemical fertilisers: nitrogen (N), phosphorus (P) and potassium (K). The nitrogen often comes from feather meal, horns and castor-oil cake, while phosphorus is provided by fish bones, natural phosphate and beet stillage. They decompose slowly and are absorbed gradually, feeding the soil, renewing its fertility and gently nourishing the plants without harming them. However, natural fertilisers must be introduced ahead of growing time, either in autumn or late winter when the soil is being prepared. Recommended dosages will be indicated on the product package and should be adhered to. More specific fertilisers can be added later in the growing cycle for demanding crops, but dried blood and guano should be avoided: their rapid action is similar to that of chemical fertilisers and they have a tendency to leach out when it rains.

Growing green manures

Green manures are sown specifically to improve the structure of the soil; to enrich and cover it so that it won't get packed when it rains, in addition to fighting some parasites and weeds. When choosing green manure crops, consider the duration of their growth cycle, their uses and the nature of your soil. Green manures find their place between the harvest of one crop and the seeding or planting of another in the same patch, if there is a long gap, for instance between spring spinach and autumn turnips. You can also use them in late summer and autumn in a bed you plan to keep fallow until next spring. In the latter case, the crop will have to be frost hardy. Green manures not killed by frost should be cut back after they bloom to make sure they don't reseed themselves, then crushed and buried. Do not plant a green manure crop of the same family as the vegetable that precedes or follows it (see table and 'Crop Rotation' p. 28).

Sweet lupin is sown from March to July (1–2 kg/100 m², 2–4 lb/100 sq yd). The white lupin prefers heavy soils, while the yellow lupin likes poor, sandy soil.

White mustard is sown from March to August (150–200 g/100 m², 4–6 oz/100 sq yd) but should not be grown immediately before or after cabbages, turnips or radishes. It is good for heavy, even limey soil and grows quickly, fighting nematodes and weeds.

Phacelia can be sown from March to August (150–200 g/100 m², 4–6 oz/100 sq yd) and should be buried two months later. Phacelia grows very quickly, fights nematodes and its flowers attract numerous pollinators. There are no vegetables in this plant family so it can be grown between any variety.

Buckwheat should be sown from May to August (500–600 g/100 m², 14–18 oz/100 sq yd) as this crop is not frost hardy. It is especially useful when used in poor acid soils to loosen soil and choke weeds.

Rye can be sown in September or October (2 kg/100 m², 4 lb/100 sq yd). Completely hardy, it should be buried in spring. Suited to poor soils on the acidic side and for fighting weeds, rye can also be grown together with vetch (500 g/1lb rye and 700 g/1½ lb vetch per 100 m² /100 sq yd). The latter's tendrils hang on to its stems, and this combination has been found to improve nitrogen content in the soil.

White clover is sown from April to September (50–100 g/100 m², 1½–3 oz/ 100 sq yd) in cold heavy soils. Dig it under in autumn and spring, and remember that this perennial can also be grown in paths.

Mulching

Another way to keep soil covered between crops is to spread mulch over empty beds. This keeps the soil cool between rainfall or watering, and slows the growth of weeds, making them easier to pull. Some mulches can also enrich or lighten soil, but **wait until the earth warms up in spring before adding them, preferably in May.**

Prepare the soil by weeding carefully and watering, before spreading a 5 cm (2 in) layer of mulch on top, which can include grass mowings, hemp or linen chaff, cocoa shells or crushed straw. The layer should be renewed regularly, as grass mowings break down particularly fast. Spread the mulch at the end of spring, and turn it in autumn.

Choosing plants and their location

Over the years, gardeners have come to notice that some plants help each other out – they are 'companions'– whereas others seem to 'dislike' each other. These affinities can be used when planning your garden, and if successfully paired, your vegetables and other plants will be stronger as a result and more resistant to parasites and disease. Taking the time to establish yearly rotations and companion plants can also help avoid the need for chemical treatments. This process becomes easier as time passes, and you will be well rewarded. Remember that some vegetables need to be pollinated, so sow them next to plants that attract honeybees.

Attracting pollinators

Bees and other pollinating insects are becoming rarer, despite their usefulness. To encourage their presence in your garden, sow or plant borage, cosmos flowers, marigolds, phacelia or calendula along garden paths and between vegetable rows. Choose simple flowers, which make foraging easier, and when planting herbs, plant more of them than you need so you can allow some to bloom. Pollinators love chives, rosemary, savoury and thyme, and as they visit them, they will also visit vegetable flowers nearby – aubergine (eggplant), cucumber, squash, strawberries, beans, peas and tomatoes – making for a more abundant harvest.

Choosing companion plants

Although it is not entirely clear how, some plants seem to encourage their neighbours' growth. This is certainly the case with borage, nasturtium, marigold, sage and sunflowers. These plants also attract pollinating insects and repel parasites, so plant them throughout your garden (see table on p. 29).

Crop rotation

The term 'crop rotation' refers to the succession of crops on the same plot of garden. It is determined by plants' own cycles, rather than by the calendar year. Here's an example of how to implement crop rotation in a vegetable garden:

Year 1: divide your vegetable garden into four squares of the same surface area. **In square 1** sow legumes such as peas and beans that contribute nitrogen to the soil. After the harvest, cut the stems so that they decompose in the ground. **In square 2** plant leaf vegetables such as cabbage, lettuce and spinach. In **square 3** plant roots: potatoes, beets, turnips and so on. **Divide square 4 in two:** keep one half fertiliser-free for undemanding plants such as bulbs (garlic, shallot, onion); in the other half, incorporate compost and plant or sow vegetables that need a rich soil, for example aubergine (eggplant), cucumber, squash, melons, tomatoes and flower crop (broccoli, cauliflower etc.).

In the following years, rotate the vegetables in the squares:

Year 2: In square 1 leaf vegetables replace legumes, benefiting from the nitrogen left behind. **In square 2** root vegetables follow leaves, looking for food deeper in the soil. **Square 3** will be divided: one half for demanding, the other half for undemanding vegetables. Cultivate legumes in **square 4**.

In years 3 and 4, keep shifting crops around the squares, always in the same order. **In year 5** cultivate the same vegetables in the same squares as in year 1.

Some plants remain in place for several seasons (perennial herbs, artichokes, asparagus, strawberries, small fruit, rhubarb etc.) on the edges of the garden and along paths. Place them a little to the north and west depending on their sun requirements, so that they won't overshadow the crops.

A few location rules

In summary, following these simple rules will help prevent deficiencies and disease:

* **Respect individual plants' preferences** regarding soil fertility (some plants are greedy, others less demanding or downright abstemious) and the acid or alkaline nature of the soil.
* **Consider 'companion planting'**– favourable or unfavourable proximities (see table on p. 29).
* **Practise crop rotation** – avoid cultivating plants of the same family in the same location two years in a row (see table below).

Green manure plants

Plant family	Herbs, grains, vegetables	Green manures
Apiaceae	carrot, celery, chervil, fennel, parsnip, parsley	
Asteraceae	artichoke, cardoon, chicory, tarragon, lettuce, salsify	
Brassica	cabbage, cress, white turnip, radish, horseradish, rocket	rape, white mustard, brassica
Chenopodiaceae	beets, spinach, Swiss chard	
Cucurbitaceae	cucumber, squash, melon, watermelon, pumpkin	
Fabaceae	beans, lentils, peas	lupin, alfalfa, sainfoin, clover, vetch

Plant family	Herbs, grains, vegetables	Green manures
Hydrophyllaceae		phacelia
Lamiaceae	basil, Chinese artichoke, mint, oregano, rosemary, sage, thyme	
Liliaceae	garlic, asparagus, chive, shallot, onion, leek	
Poaceae	oats, wheat, corn, barley, rye	oat, rye
Polygonaceae	sorrel, rhubarb	buckwheat
Solanaceae	aubergine (eggplant), pepper, potato, tomato	

Companion planting

As discussed, plants influence each other when grown together; some encourage growth, while others dislike being in close proximity. It is well known that leeks keep away the carrot fly, the proximity of carrots discourages leek moths, and radishes are sweeter when grown near lettuce. The table below will help you to discover other associations and which crops to separate.

✓: friends ✗: enemies

	asparagus	aubergine (eggplant)	beet(root)	broad bean (fava)	cabbage	carrot	celery	cucumber	garlic	green bean	leek	lettuce	melon	onion	pea	potato	squash/pumpkin	radish	shallot	spinach	marrow/courgette	strawberry	tomato	turnip
asparagus						✓	✓	✓	✓	✓	✓				✓								✓	
aubergine (eggplant)										✓								✓	✓					
beet(root)				✓	✗	✓			✓	✓	✗	✓		✓		✗		✓	✓	✓			✗	
broad bean (fava)					✓	✓	✓	✓	✗	✓	✗	✓		✗	✗	✓		✓	✗	✓	✓			
cabbage			✓	✓		✓	✓	✓		✓		✓		✗	✓	✓		✗	✗	✓		✗		
carrot		✗	✓	✓	✓			✓		✓	✓	✓		✓	✓	✗		✓	✓	✓			✓	
celery			✓	✓	✓	✓		✓		✓	✓	✗		✓	✗			✓					✓	
cucumber	✓			✓	✓		✓			✓		✓	✗	✓	✓			✓					✗	
garlic	✓		✓	✗	✓					✗	✗	✓		✗	✓							✓	✓	
green bean	✓	✓	✓	✓	✓	✓	✓	✓	✗		✗	✓	✓	✗	✗	✓		✓	✗	✓	✓	✓		✓
leek	✓		✗	✗	✓	✓			✗			✓		✓	✗	✗		✓				✓	✓	
lettuce	✓		✓	✓	✓	✓	✗	✓	✓	✓	✓		✓	✓	✓			✓	✓	✓	✓	✓		✓
melon						✗		✓		✓				✓	✗						✓	✗		
onion			✓	✗	✗	✓			✗	✓	✓				✗	✗		✓				✓	✓	✗
pea	✓			✗	✓	✓	✓	✓	✗	✗	✗	✓	✓	✗		✓		✓	✗	✓			✗	✓
potato			✗	✓	✓	✗	✗	✗	✓	✓				✗	✗		✗	✓			✗		✗	
squash/pumpkin		✓														✗		✓					✓	
radish		✓	✓	✓	✗	✓	✓			✓		✓		✓					✓		✗		✓	
shallot			✓	✗	✗	✓			✗			✓		✓	✗	✓						✓	✓	
spinach			✓	✓	✓	✓				✓	✓	✓	✓	✓				✓				✓	✓	✓
marrow/courgette		✓								✓		✓	✓	✗	✓		✗	✗					✗	
strawberry				✗			✓	✓	✓	✓		✓		✓				✓	✓					✓
tomato	✓	✗		✓	✓	✗	✓		✓					✗	✗			✓	✓	✓	✗			✓
turnip						✓		✓				✗	✓					✓			✓			

Fighting disease and parasites

Don't reach for the spray pump the minute you spot aphids or powdery mildew. Take preventive action by encouraging the development of helpful insects, introducing companion plants whose fragrance repels parasites, or using plant-based preparations. Pesticides should only be used as a last resort.

Encouraging helpful insects

Learn to recognise not only adult insects but also their eggs and larvae, so as not to destroy them mistakenly. Ladybirds, hoverflies and lacewings are your allies and will devour aphids. If you plant nectar-rich flowers and provide natural or manmade shelters where they can spend the winter, these helpful creatures will be ready for action as soon as the first pests appear in spring. Most importantly, use chemical treatments as little as possible. If aphids appear before their predators, cut back the affected parts of the plant, giving the helpful insects time to develop ahead of the next generation of pests.

Making plant preparations

Herbal preparations are made by macerating certain plants before they go to seed and spraying the resulting 'tea' to fight disease or parasites. Always use rainwater and wooden containers (never metal), preferably closed, to mix preparations. Since these liquids do not keep very long, be ready to prepare several batches in the course of a growing season.

Two techniques are used: manures (or macerations) and teas (or decoctions). **For manures**, soak the plants in cold water until all soluble substances are dissolved, then filter and dilute the manure before use. You can use ferns to fight aphids and slugs; nettles against aphids and various diseases; and elder to fight flea beetles, aphids and thrips, and to prevent as well as fight cabbage white butterflies and leek moths. **For teas**, soak plants for an entire day, then boil over a low heat for 20 minutes, allow to cool, then filter for use. Horsetail is good for all diseases, while tansy is effective for aphids, cutworms and cabbage white butterflies.

Recipes

Nettle manure

Macerate 1 kg (2 lb) fresh, chopped nettles in 10 l (qt) rain water for 4–5 days. Filter and dilute to 20% (2 parts manure to 10 parts water) before spraying.

Elder manure

Chop 1 kg (2 lb) elder leaves, flowers, fruit and young stems. Soak in 10 l (qt) water for 3 days. Filter but don't dilute.

Horsetail tea

Cut 200 g (8 oz) fresh horsetail leaves and mix with 10 l (qt) water. Soak for 1 day before boiling for 20 minutes. Let it rest for 24 hours, then filter before spraying.

Establishing insect-repellent plants

The smell of many plants' leaves repels parasites and some diseases. Other plants attract them, pulling them away from neighbouring vegetables or ornamental plants. Below is a table of approximately 20 plant-allies and the parasites and diseases they fight.

Helpful plants	Use for	Plant near
Garlic, chives, shallots, onion	blister beetle flies	peach tree carrot
Lovage	flea beetle aphids	cabbage, turnip, radish beans, lettuce, tomato
Basil	mildew	cucumber, squash
Borage	cabbage white butterfly	cabbage
Nasturtium	whitefly mildew aphids	aubergine (eggplant), cabbage, cucumber, tomato tomato cabbage, cucumber, squash, beans, lettuce, pepper, roses, tomato
Chives	Japanese beetle flies	potato carrot
Coriander (cilantro)	flea beetle Japanese beetle flies	beets, cabbage, turnip, radish potato carrot
Cosmos	cabbage white butterfly	cabbage
Lettuce	flea beetle	cabbage, turnip, radish
Lavender	aphids	roses
Mint	flea beetle cabbage white butterfly	cabbage, turnip radish cabbage
French marigold	whitefly flea beetle nematodes cabbage white butterfly aphids	aubergine (eggplant), cabbage, cucumber, tomato cabbage, turnip, radish tomato cabbage cucumber, squash, spinach, beans, pepper
Parsley	flies aphids	carrot, onion melon, tomato
Horseradish	Japanese beetle rust	potato celery
Rosemary	flea beetle flies cabbage white butterfly aphids	cabbage, turnip, radish carrot, bean cabbage beans, lettuce
Savory	flea beetle flies cabbage white butterfly aphids	cabbage, turnip, radish beans cabbage beans, lettuce
Sage	flea beetle flies cabbage white butterfly aphids	cabbage, turnip, radish carrot cabbage cucumber, squash, lettuce
Common marigold	whitefly nematodes aphids	aubergine (eggplant), cabbage, cucumber, tomato tomato squash, spinach, lettuce, beans, peppers
Tobacco	whitefly thrips	aubergine (eggplant), cabbage, cucumber, tomato gladiolus, pea
Thyme	flea beetle slugs cabbage white butterfly	cabbage, turnip, radish squash, spinach, lettuce, melon cabbage
Tomato	flea beetle	cabbage, turnip, radish

Designing your Garden

You can use the space below to design your garden. If your growing space is small, draw the layout of your March–April crops on the left and your June–July crops on the right, after you have harvested the spring yield.

Indicate where the north lies in relation to your garden. Include unchanging elements such as walls, hedges, paths, cold frames, perennials, fruit trees, herbs, asparagus and artichokes. If these aren't in place yet, indicate where they will be, and pay attention to any tall, overshadowing plants.

Divide the remaining surface into four equally-sized sections, which will each be occupied by one of the four main categories of vegetable: root, leaf, flower, seed and fruit (see p. 21). Plan the location of your winter crops according to the rules of crop rotation, companion planting and integrating flowers, indicating where the beds will be. When the time is right, just follow your plans and sow or plant your seedlings.

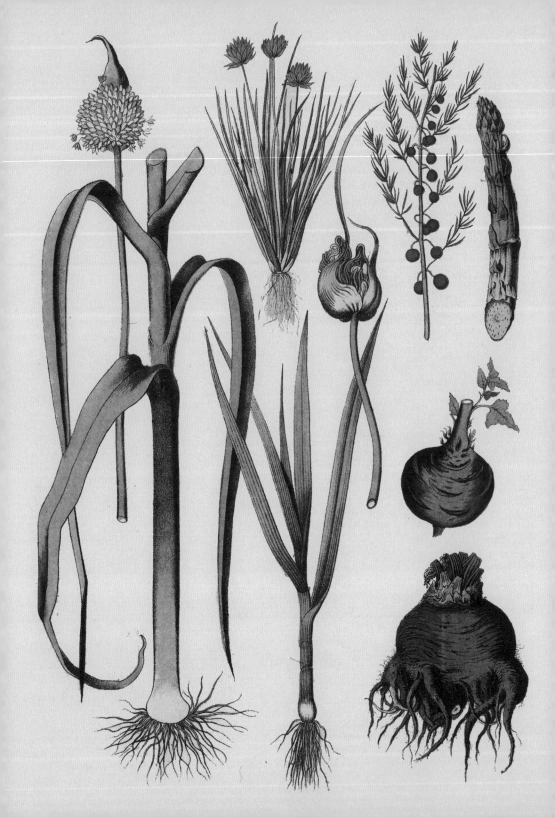

2019
Calendar

How to Use the Calendar

On the following pages, you will find a calendar for the Northern hemisphere and Greenwich Mean Time. It takes into account the main influences from the cosmos, as described in the chapter 'The Moon and the Garden' (pp. 8–33). The vegetables and plants listed are chosen as examples that suit the average growing conditions in France, and can be varied according to your taste, the climate of your garden and its latitude and altitude. Each day we suggest example tasks for tending to leaves, roots, flowers or fruit, according to season, the position of the Sun, and the position of the Moon (ascending or descending in front of particular constellations). You will have to protect your crops from the cold or the heat depending on the climate of your garden and the time of year. The examples given match an *average* climate in France. Take into account your own climate, jumping ahead or postponing tasks as compared to the calendar. If you have frost, delay all planting, pruning and treatments.

Note

It is not always possible – for personal or climatic reasons – to choose the best moment to perform particular gardening tasks. The main consideration should be the motion of the Moon – **always sow when the Moon is ascending, plant and prune when the Moon is descending.**

We have included a blank page every two weeks for you to keep a daily journal. Note everything you do in the garden: which variety of carrots or beans you sow, which day the lettuce came up, when you picked the first tomatoes or beans, when the almond tree blossomed, and when the first cuckoo sang. Don't hesitate to include birthdays. Does someone like a particular plant? Make a note in your calendar to sow or plant this flower at the right time so you can give them a cutting. Your notes will help you to progress your gardening skills and knowledge, and the more notes you take, the more pleasure you will have consulting them.

Remember, all times are given in GMT. If you are not in Britain or Ireland, you need to adjust for your time zone (see p. 37).

Crop tables

You may prefer to plan your tasks differently. Make a list of the plants you want to cultivate and then create a personal calendar of your gardening with the Moon. The crop table on pp. 106–15 offers a range of possibilities.

Calendar key

⊙	the Sun
⊙ ♐	eg. the Sun is in Sagittarius (see p. 18 for constellation symbols)
●	new Moon
◖	first quarter Moon
○	full Moon
◗	last quarter Moon
☊	ascending Moon node
☋	descending Moon node

Note: Do not confuse ascending or descending Moon nodes with the ascending or descending Moon.

Local Times

Times given are *Greenwich Mean Time* (GMT), using 24-hour clock, e.g. 3pm is written 15:00. **No account is taken of daylight saving (summer) time (DST).** Note 00:00 is midnight at the beginning of a date, and 24:00 is midnight at the end of the date. Add (+) or subtract (−) times as below. For countries not listed check local time against GMT.

Europe

Britain, Ireland, Portugal: GMT
(March 31 to Oct 26, +1^h for DST)
Iceland: GMT (no DST)
Central Europe: +1^h
(March 31 to Oct 26, +2^h for DST)
Eastern Europe (Finland, etc.): +2^h
(March 31 to Oct 26, +3^h for DST)
Russia (Moscow) +3^h (no DST)
Georgia: +4^h (no DST)

Africa/Asia

Egypt: add 2^h (no DST)
Israel: add 2^h (March 29 to Oct 26,
+3^h for DST)
India: add 5½^h (no DST)
Philippines, China: add 8^h (no DST)
Japan, Korea: add 9^h (no DST)

North America

Newfoundland Standard Time: − 3½^h
(March 10 to Nov 2, − 2½^h for DST)
Atlantic Standard Time: − 4^h
(March 10 to Nov 2, − 3^h for DST)
Eastern Standard Time: − 5^h
(March 10 to Nov 2, − 4^h for DST)
Central Standard Time: − 6^h
(except Saskatchewan March 10 to Nov 2,
− 5^h for DST)
Mountain Standard Time: − 7^h (except AZ,
March 10 to Nov 2, − 6^h for DST)
Pacific Standard Time: − 8^h
(March 10 to Nov 2, − 7^h for DST)
Alaska Standard Time: − 9^h
(March 10 to Nov 2, − 8^h for DST)
Hawaii Standard Time: − 10^h
(no DST)
Mexico (CST): −6^h
(April 7 to Oct 26, −5^h for DST)

January 2019

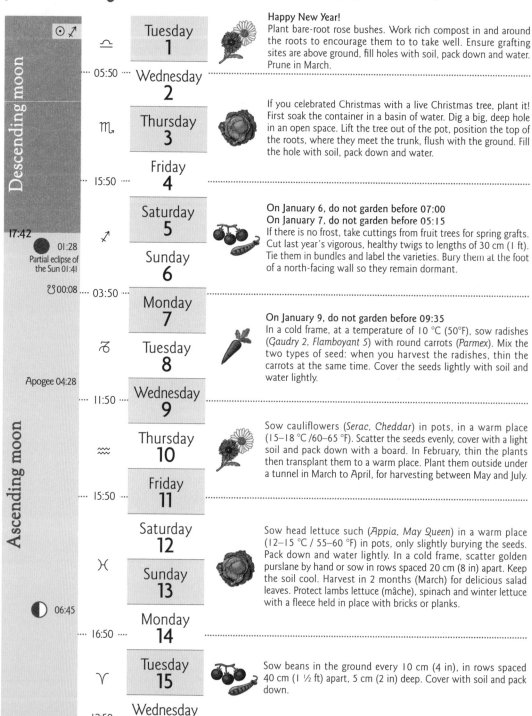

Descending moon

☉ ♐

♎ **Tuesday 1**

Happy New Year!
Plant bare-root rose bushes. Work rich compost in and around the roots to encourage them to to take well. Ensure grafting sites are above ground, fill holes with soil, pack down and water. Prune in March.

···· 05:50 ···· **Wednesday 2**

♏ **Thursday 3**

If you celebrated Christmas with a live Christmas tree, plant it! First soak the container in a basin of water. Dig a big, deep hole in an open space. Lift the tree out of the pot, position the top of the roots, where they meet the trunk, flush with the ground. Fill the hole with soil, pack down and water.

Friday 4

···· 15:50 ····

Saturday 5

On January 6, do not garden before 07:00
On January 7, do not garden before 05:15
If there is no frost, take cuttings from fruit trees for spring grafts. Cut last year's vigorous, healthy twigs to lengths of 30 cm (1 ft). Tie them in bundles and label the varieties. Bury them at the foot of a north-facing wall so they remain dormant.

♐ 17:42 ● 01:28
Partial eclipse of the Sun 01:41

Sunday 6

☊ 00:08 ···· 03:50 ····

Monday 7

On January 9, do not garden before 09:35
In a cold frame, at a temperature of 10 °C (50°F), sow radishes (*Gaudry 2, Flamboyant 5*) with round carrots (*Parmex*). Mix the two types of seed: when you harvest the radishes, thin the carrots at the same time. Cover the seeds lightly with soil and water lightly.

♑ **Tuesday 8**

Apogee 04:28

···· 11:50 ···· **Wednesday 9**

Ascending moon

♒ **Thursday 10**

Sow cauliflowers (*Serac, Cheddar*) in pots, in a warm place (15–18 °C /60–65 °F). Scatter the seeds evenly, cover with a light soil and pack down with a board. In February, thin the plants then transplant them to a warm place. Plant them outside under a tunnel in March to April, for harvesting between May and July.

···· 15:50 ···· **Friday 11**

Saturday 12

Sow head lettuce such (*Appia, May Queen*) in a warm place (12–15 °C / 55–60 °F) in pots, only slightly burying the seeds. Pack down and water lightly. In a cold frame, scatter golden purslane by hand or sow in rows spaced 20 cm (8 in) apart. Keep the soil cool. Harvest in 2 months (March) for delicious salad leaves. Protect lambs lettuce (mâche), spinach and winter lettuce with a fleece held in place with bricks or planks.

♓ **Sunday 13**

◑ 06:45

Monday 14

···· 16:50 ····

♈ **Tuesday 15**

Sow beans in the ground every 10 cm (4 in), in rows spaced 40 cm (1 ½ ft) apart, 5 cm (2 in) deep. Cover with soil and pack down.

···· 12:50 ···· **Wednesday 16**

Your notes and observations

January 2019

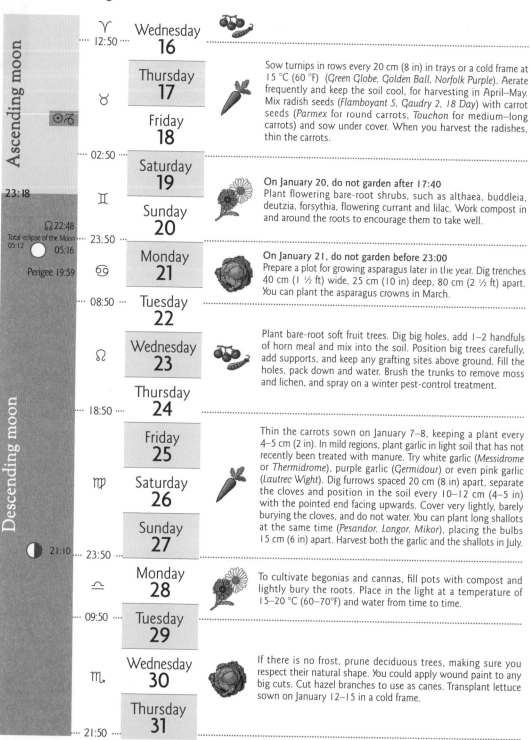

Ascending moon

♈ ···· 12:50 ····
Wednesday
16

☉⅞

♉
Thursday
17

Friday
18

···· 02:50 ····
Saturday
19

23:18

♊
Sunday
20

☊ 22:48

Total eclipse of the Moon
05:12 ○ 05:16

···· 23:50 ····
Monday
21

Perigee 19:59 ♋

Tuesday
22

···· 08:50 ····

Descending moon

♌
Wednesday
23

Thursday
24

···· 18:50 ····
Friday
25

♍
Saturday
26

Sunday
27

☽ 21:10 ···· 23:50 ····
Monday
28

♎
Tuesday
29

···· 09:50 ····

♏
Wednesday
30

Thursday
31

···· 21:50 ····

Sow turnips in rows every 20 cm (8 in) in trays or a cold frame at 15 °C (60 °F) (*Green Globe, Golden Ball, Norfolk Purple*). Aerate frequently and keep the soil cool, for harvesting in April–May. Mix radish seeds (*Flamboyant 5, Gaudry 2, 18 Day*) with carrot seeds (*Parmex* for round carrots, *Touchon* for medium–long carrots) and sow under cover. When you harvest the radishes, thin the carrots.

On January 20, do not garden after 17:40
Plant flowering bare-root shrubs, such as althaea, buddleia, deutzia, forsythia, flowering currant and lilac. Work compost in and around the roots to encourage them to take well.

On January 21, do not garden before 23:00
Prepare a plot for growing asparagus later in the year. Dig trenches 40 cm (1 ½ ft) wide, 25 cm (10 in) deep, 80 cm (2 ½ ft) apart. You can plant the asparagus crowns in March.

Plant bare-root soft fruit trees. Dig big holes, add 1–2 handfuls of horn meal and mix into the soil. Position big trees carefully, add supports, and keep any grafting sites above ground. Fill the holes, pack down and water. Brush the trunks to remove moss and lichen, and spray on a winter pest-control treatment.

Thin the carrots sown on January 7–8, keeping a plant every 4–5 cm (2 in). In mild regions, plant garlic in light soil that has not recently been treated with manure. Try white garlic (*Messidrome* or *Thermidrome*), purple garlic (*Germidour*) or even pink garlic (*Lautrec Wight*). Dig furrows spaced 20 cm (8 in) apart, separate the cloves and position in the soil every 10–12 cm (4–5 in) with the pointed end facing upwards. Cover very lightly, barely burying the cloves, and do not water. You can plant long shallots at the same time (*Pesandor, Longor, Mikor*), placing the bulbs 15 cm (6 in) apart. Harvest both the garlic and the shallots in July.

To cultivate begonias and cannas, fill pots with compost and lightly bury the roots. Place in the light at a temperature of 15–20 °C (60–70°F) and water from time to time.

If there is no frost, prune deciduous trees, making sure you respect their natural shape. You could apply wound paint to any big cuts. Cut hazel branches to use as canes. Transplant lettuce sown on January 12–15 in a cold frame.

Your notes and observations

February 2019

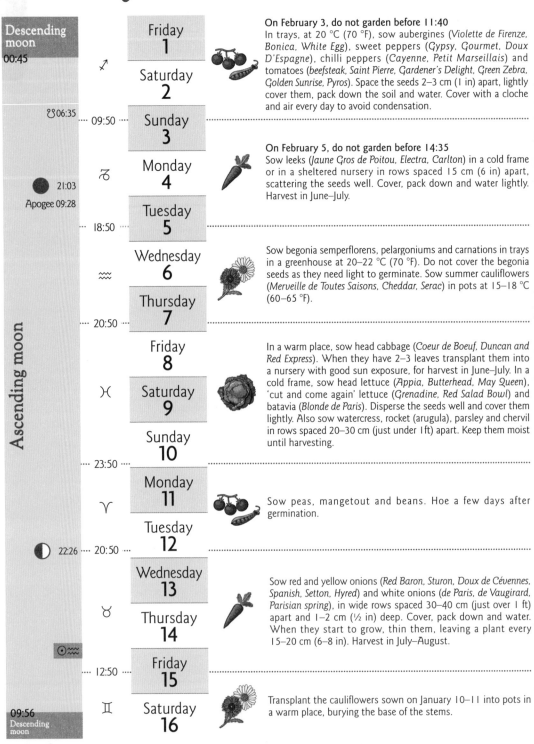

Descending moon 00:45

☊ 06:35 ···· 09:50 ····

● 21:03
Apogee 09:28

···· 18:50 ····

···· 20:50 ····

···· 23:50 ····

◑ 22:26 ···· 20:50 ····

···· 12:50 ····

09:56
Descending moon

Ascending moon

♐
♑
♒
♓
♈
♉ ☉♒
♊

Friday 1

Saturday 2

Sunday 3

Monday 4

Tuesday 5

Wednesday 6

Thursday 7

Friday 8

Saturday 9

Sunday 10

Monday 11

Tuesday 12

Wednesday 13

Thursday 14

Friday 15

Saturday 16

On February 3, do not garden before 11:40
In trays, at 20 °C (70 °F), sow aubergines (*Violette de Firenze, Bonica, White Egg*), sweet peppers (*Gypsy, Gourmet, Doux D'Espagne*), chilli peppers (*Cayenne, Petit Marseillais*) and tomatoes (*beefsteak, Saint Pierre, Gardener's Delight, Green Zebra, Golden Sunrise, Pyros*). Space the seeds 2–3 cm (1 in) apart, lightly cover them, pack down the soil and water. Cover with a cloche and air every day to avoid condensation.

On February 5, do not garden before 14:35
Sow leeks (*Jaune Gros de Poitou, Electra, Carlton*) in a cold frame or in a sheltered nursery in rows spaced 15 cm (6 in) apart, scattering the seeds well. Cover, pack down and water lightly. Harvest in June–July.

Sow begonia semperflorens, pelargoniums and carnations in trays in a greenhouse at 20–22 °C (70 °F). Do not cover the begonia seeds as they need light to germinate. Sow summer cauliflowers (*Merveille de Toutes Saisons, Cheddar, Serac*) in pots at 15–18 °C (60–65 °F).

In a warm place, sow head cabbage (*Coeur de Boeuf, Duncan and Red Express*). When they have 2–3 leaves transplant them into a nursery with good sun exposure, for harvest in June–July. In a cold frame, sow head lettuce (*Appia, Butterhead, May Queen*), 'cut and come again' lettuce (*Grenadine, Red Salad Bowl*) and batavia (*Blonde de Paris*). Disperse the seeds well and cover them lightly. Also sow watercress, rocket (arugula), parsley and chervil in rows spaced 20–30 cm (just under 1ft) apart. Keep them moist until harvesting.

Sow peas, mangetout and beans. Hoe a few days after germination.

Sow red and yellow onions (*Red Baron, Sturon, Doux de Cévennes, Spanish, Setton, Hyred*) and white onions (*de Paris, de Vaugirard, Parisian spring*), in wide rows spaced 30–40 cm (just over 1 ft) apart and 1–2 cm (½ in) deep. Cover, pack down and water. When they start to grow, thin them, leaving a plant every 15–20 cm (6–8 in). Harvest in July–August.

Transplant the cauliflowers sown on January 10–11 into pots in a warm place, burying the base of the stems.

Your notes and observations

February 2019

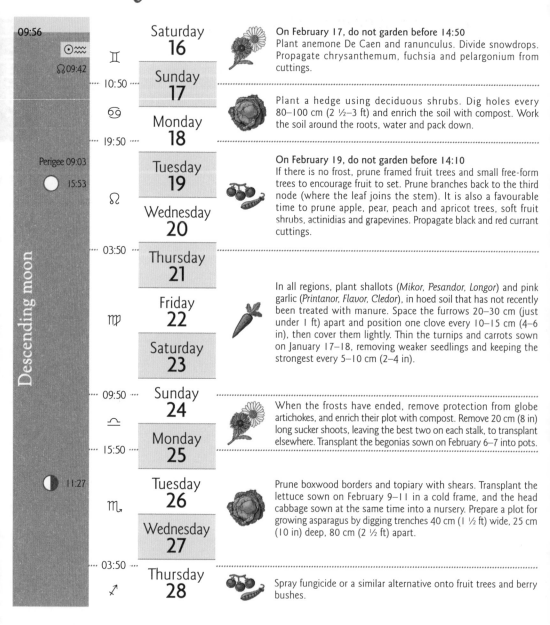

09:56

☉ ♒

☊ 09:42

♊

Saturday
16

···· 10:50 ····

Sunday
17

On February 17, do not garden before 14:50
Plant anemone De Caen and ranunculus. Divide snowdrops. Propagate chrysanthemum, fuchsia and pelargonium from cuttings.

♋

Monday
18

···· 19:50 ····

Plant a hedge using deciduous shrubs. Dig holes every 80–100 cm (2 ½–3 ft) and enrich the soil with compost. Work the soil around the roots, water and pack down.

Perigee 09:03

○ 15:53

♌

Tuesday
19

Wednesday
20

On February 19, do not garden before 14:10
If there is no frost, prune framed fruit trees and small free-form trees to encourage fruit to set. Prune branches back to the third node (where the leaf joins the stem). It is also a favourable time to prune apple, pear, peach and apricot trees, soft fruit shrubs, actinidias and grapevines. Propagate black and red currant cuttings.

···· 03:50 ····

Thursday
21

Friday
22

♍

In all regions, plant shallots (*Mikor, Pesandor, Longor*) and pink garlic (*Printanor, Flavor, Cledor*), in hoed soil that has not recently been treated with manure. Space the furrows 20–30 cm (just under 1 ft) apart and position one clove every 10–15 cm (4–6 in), then cover them lightly. Thin the turnips and carrots sown on January 17–18, removing weaker seedlings and keeping the strongest every 5–10 cm (2–4 in).

Saturday
23

···· 09:50 ····

Sunday
24

♎

When the frosts have ended, remove protection from globe artichokes, and enrich their plot with compost. Remove 20 cm (8 in) long sucker shoots, leaving the best two on each stalk, to transplant elsewhere. Transplant the begonias sown on February 6–7 into pots.

Monday
25

···· 15:50 ····

◐ 11:27

♏

Tuesday
26

Prune boxwood borders and topiary with shears. Transplant the lettuce sown on February 9–11 in a cold frame, and the head cabbage sown at the same time into a nursery. Prepare a plot for growing asparagus by digging trenches 40 cm (1 ½ ft) wide, 25 cm (10 in) deep, 80 cm (2 ½ ft) apart.

Wednesday
27

···· 03:50 ····

Thursday
28

♐

Spray fungicide or a similar alternative onto fruit trees and berry bushes.

Descending moon

Your notes and observations

March 2019

06:17

Ascending moon

♐

♉ 11:03 — 15:50

♑

Apogee 11:26

— 00:50

≈

● 16:03

— 02:50

♓

— 05:50

♈

☉♓

— 02:50

♉

◐ 10:27

♊

18:02
Descending moon
♌ 16:22 — 19:50

| | Friday **1** |
| Saturday **2** |

On March 2, do not garden before 16:10
In pots or in beds, at 18–20 °C (65–70 °F), sow tomatoes (*beefsteak, Saint Pierre, Pyros*), aubergines (*Violette de Firenze, Bonica, White Egg*), sweet peppers (*Gypsy, Gourmet, Doux D'Espagne*) and chilli peppers (*Cayenne, Petit Marseillais*). Graft fruit trees using the cuttings taken on 5–6 January.

| Sunday **3** |
| Monday **4** |

On March 4, do not garden before 16:35
Sew medium-long carrots (*Touchon, Nanco, Valor*) and radishes (*Gaudry 2, Flamboyant 5, 18 Day*) in a cold frame or a plot with good sun exposure, in rows spaced 20–30 cm (just under 1 ft) apart. Mix the two seeds: when you harvest the radishes, thin the carrots at the same time.

| Tuesday **5** |
| Wednesday **6** |

Fill a pot with finely sifted compost and pack down with a board. Scatter Busy Lizzie (impatiens) seeds on the surface and tap down again without covering the seeds. Spray with water, cover with a cloche and place in a warm spot. In a nursery well exposed to the sun, sow summer cauliflower (*Serac, Cheddar*) and Romanesco broccoli, for transplanting in a month's time, with seedlings spaced 10 cm (4 in) apart.

| Thursday **7** |
| Friday **8** |
| Saturday **9** |

Like every month when the moon is in Pisces (*Poissons*) sow head lettuce (*Appia, Butterhead, May Queen*), batavia (*Blonde de Paris*), 'cut and come again' (*Grenadine, Red Salad Bowl*) or Romaine lettuce in beds or in the nursery. Scatter seeds well, pack down and water. Sow spring spinach (*Palco, Junius, America, Viking*) in beds. You can also sow dandelions, cress, rocket (arugula), parsley and chervil, in rows spaced 20–30 cm (just under 1 ft) apart. Keep the soil damp until they sprout.

| Sunday **10** |
| Monday **11** |

Sow cucumbers, melon and physalis in a warm place at 20–25 °C (70–77 °F).

| Tuesday **12** |
| Wednesday **13** |
| Thursday **14** |

In a warm place (18–20 °C / 70–65 °F), in trays filled with a light compost, sow Monarch celeriac. Cover the seeds lightly, pack down with a board and keep the soil damp until they sprout. In the nursery, sow leeks for autumn harvest (*Jaune gros du Poitou, Malabar, Pancho, Hannibal*) in rows spaced 20 cm (8 in) apart, 1–2 cm (½–1 in) deep. Thin the seedlings after germination, every 5 cm (2 in).

| Friday **15** |
| Saturday **16** |

On March 16, do not garden after 11:15
Prune climbing roses, cutting branches back by one third of their length, and bushes to a height of 30 cm (1 ft) from the ground. Remove the old stems. Transplant the cauliflowers sown on February 6–7 into pots.

Your notes and observations

March 2019

♊   ☊ 16:22

Saturday 16

19:50

On March 16, do not garden after 11:15
Transplant the pelargoniums and begonias sown on February 6–7 into pots. Remove sucker shoots from globe artichokes.

♋

Sunday 17

Space asparagus crowns at least 30cm (1ft) apart on a ridge of soil in a trench. Spread the roots evenly and fill the trench with soil, burying the roots 5 cm (2 in) deep. Water. Plant evergreen shrubs in containers.

06:50

Monday 18

Perigee 19:47

♌

Tuesday 19

On March 19, do not garden after 14:40
Finish pruning fruit trees and grapevines. Prune peach and olive trees as they start to flower, removing some growth to let in air and light and to encourage fruit growth. Transplant the aubergines, chilli peppers, peppers and tomatoes sown February 1–2 into pots. Hoe the peas sown on February 12, supporting climbing varieties.

Spring Equinox 21:58

○ 01:42

14:50

Wednesday 20

Thursday 21

Plant early germinating potatoes (*Charlotte, Abbot, Maris Bard*). Rows should be 80 cm (2 ½ ft) apart, with potatoes planted 35 cm (14 in) apart and 10 cm (4 in) deep with shoots facing upwards. When the leaves are 25 cm (10 in) tall, earth them up. Also plant Chinese and Jerusalem artichokes and horseradish bought or saved from last year. Thin the carrots sown on March 3–4.

♍

Friday 22

Saturday 23

17:50

♎

Sunday 24

Prune seasonal flowering shrubs. Cut the branches back to 4–5 cm (2 in) above the ground or frame. Plant the cauliflowers sown on January 10–11 under cover. Thin the impatiens sown March 5–6 every 5 cm (2 in).

00:50

Monday 25

♏

Tuesday 26

Plant the head cabbage sown on February 9–11 and the lettuce sown on March 8–10. Blanch dandelions. Thin the spinach sown on March 8–10. Plant or divide chives, tarragon, sorrel and rhubarb, adding compost.

10:50

Wednesday 27

◐ 04:09

12:55

♐

Thursday 28

On March 29, do not garden after 08:00
Sow peas (*Kelvedon Wonder, Balmoral, Dorian, Douce Provence*), mangetout and sugar snaps (*Oregon Sugar Pod, Cascadia*) and broad beans/fava (*Seville longpods, Aguadulce*) in rows spaced 30–40 cm (just over 1 ft) apart, 5 cm (2 in) deep. Hoe after germination.

☊ 13:08

Friday 29

21:50

Saturday 30

♑

Sow carrots (*Adelaide, Flyaway, Parmex*) in rows spaced 30 cm (1 ft) apart, 2 cm (1 in) deep. Pack down and water. Sow radishes (*Gaudry 2, Flamboyant 5, National 2*) and in wide furrows sow beets (*Detroit 2*).

Sunday 31

Apogee 23:21

Your notes and observations

April 2019

In UK/Ireland add 1 hour for BST

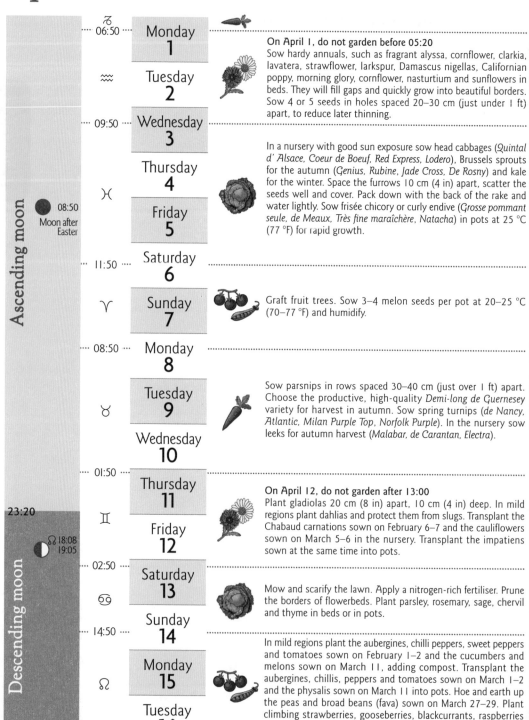

Ascending moon

♑ 06:50 — **Monday 1**

≈ **Tuesday 2**

09:50 — **Wednesday 3**

Thursday 4

⊕ 08:50
Moon after
Easter

♓ **Friday 5**

11:50 — **Saturday 6**

♈ **Sunday 7**

08:50 — **Monday 8**

♉ **Tuesday 9**

Wednesday 10

01:50 — **Thursday 11**

23:20

♊ **Friday 12**

☽ 18:08
19:05

Descending moon

02:50 — **Saturday 13**

♋ **Sunday 14**

14:50 — **Monday 15**

♌

Perigee 22:04 — 23:50 — **Tuesday 16**

On April 1, do not garden before 05:20
Sow hardy annuals, such as fragrant alyssa, cornflower, clarkia, lavatera, strawflower, larkspur, Damascus nigellas, Californian poppy, morning glory, cornflower, nasturtium and sunflowers in beds. They will fill gaps and quickly grow into beautiful borders. Sow 4 or 5 seeds in holes spaced 20–30 cm (just under 1 ft) apart, to reduce later thinning.

In a nursery with good sun exposure sow head cabbages (*Quintal d' Alsace, Coeur de Boeuf, Red Express, Lodero*), Brussels sprouts for the autumn (*Genius, Rubine, Jade Cross, De Rosny*) and kale for the winter. Space the furrows 10 cm (4 in) apart, scatter the seeds well and cover. Pack down with the back of the rake and water lightly. Sow frisée chicory or curly endive (*Grosse pommant seule, de Meaux, Très fine maraîchère, Natacha*) in pots at 25 °C (77 °F) for rapid growth.

Graft fruit trees. Sow 3–4 melon seeds per pot at 20–25 °C (70–77 °F) and humidify.

Sow parsnips in rows spaced 30–40 cm (just over 1 ft) apart. Choose the productive, high-quality *Demi-long de Guernesey* variety for harvest in autumn. Sow spring turnips (*de Nancy, Atlantic, Milan Purple Top, Norfolk Purple*). In the nursery sow leeks for autumn harvest (*Malabar, de Carantan, Electra*).

On April 12, do not garden after 13:00
Plant gladiolas 20 cm (8 in) apart, 10 cm (4 in) deep. In mild regions plant dahlias and protect them from slugs. Transplant the Chabaud carnations sown on February 6–7 and the cauliflowers sown on March 5–6 in the nursery. Transplant the impatiens sown at the same time into pots.

Mow and scarify the lawn. Apply a nitrogen-rich fertiliser. Prune the borders of flowerbeds. Plant parsley, rosemary, sage, chervil and thyme in beds or in pots.

In mild regions plant the aubergines, chilli peppers, sweet peppers and tomatoes sown on February 1–2 and the cucumbers and melons sown on March 11, adding compost. Transplant the aubergines, chillis, peppers and tomatoes sown on March 1–2 and the physalis sown on March 11 into pots. Hoe and earth up the peas and broad beans (fava) sown on March 27–29. Plant climbing strawberries, gooseberries, blackcurrants, raspberries and, in acid soil, myrtle. Water copiously.

Your notes and observations

April 2019

Descending moon

Perigee 22:04

♌

Tuesday **16**

23:50

Wednesday **17**

♍

Thursday **18**

☉♈ 11:12

Friday **19**

03:50

Saturday **20**

♎

Sunday **21**

10:50

Monday **22**

♏

Tuesday **23**

19:50

21:17

Wednesday **24**

♐

☍ 15:01

Thursday **25**

05:50

Ascending moon

◑ 22:18

Friday **26**

♑

Saturday **27**

Apogee 18:19   14:50

Sunday **28**

♒

Monday **29**

16:50

♓

Tuesday **30**

On April 17, do no garden before 03:10
When the lilac flowers plant potatoes (*Charlotte, Désirée, Sirtema, Ditta, Nicola, Roseval*). Earth them up when the foliage is around 25 cm (10 in) high. Plant the leeks sown on February 4–5 in rows spaced 30 cm (1 ft) apart, every 10 cm (4 in). Transplant the celeriac sown on March 12–14 for the first time. Thin the beets and carrots sown on March 30–31.

Plant perennials and flowering shrubs. Prune forsythia, Japanese quince and flowering currants that have finished flowering. Remove old or weak branches and dead wood. Plant the cauliflowers sown on February 6–7.

When the chicory and endive sown on April 4–6 has 5 strong leaves, transplant it under cover. Space each plant 10 cm (4 in) apart in every direction, and aerate often. In the nursery, plant the head cabbage and Brussels sprouts sown on the same date, burying their bases.

On April 25, do not garden before 09:55
Sow courgette (zucchini), marrow or squash in pots of acid-rich compost: 3 seeds per pot, 1 cm (½ in) deep, at 18–20 °C (65–70 °F) in a light position but without direct sun. Keep the best plant of each batch, for planting mid-May and harvesting from July. Sow pea seeds (*Kelvedon Wonder*).

On April 28, do not garden before 13:10
In wide rows, 20 cm (8 in) apart, sow turnips (Green Globe, Golden Ball) to be harvested two months later. Next to the leeks, sow carrots (*Lisse de Meaux, Jaune du Doubs, Nanco, Touchon*) to fight flies and ringworm.

Sow fragrant alyssa, morning glory, cornflower, nasturtium, clarkia, lavatera, larkspur, Damascus nigella, Californian poppy and sunflowers directly in the ground. Plant the seeds in holes and cover lightly. Pack down with the back of a rake and water lightly.

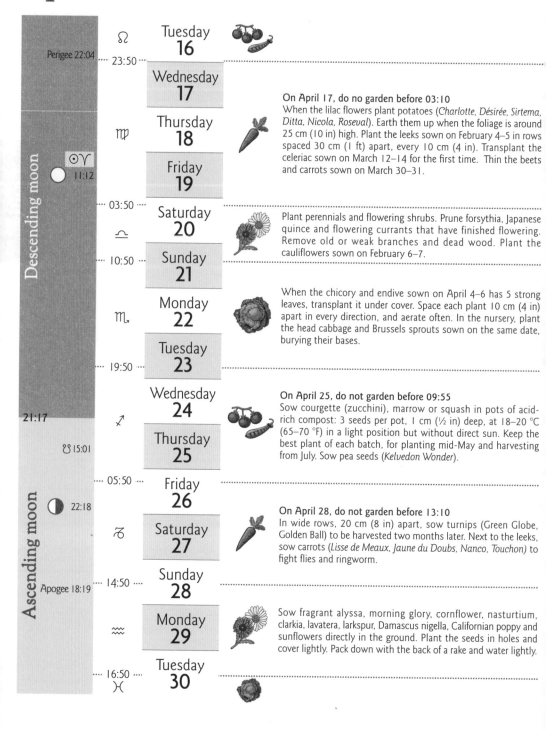

Your notes and observations

May 2019

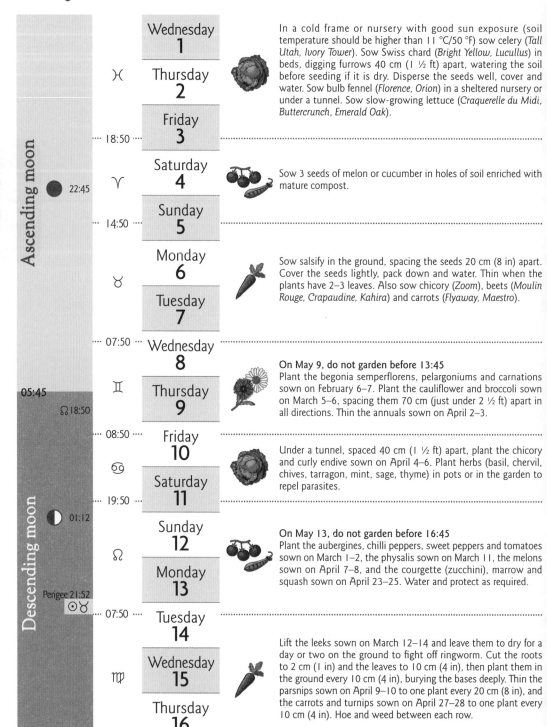

Ascending moon

Wednesday 1

ℋ **Thursday 2**

···· 18:50 ····

Friday 3

● 22:45 ♈ **Saturday 4**

···· 14:50 ····

Sunday 5

♉ **Monday 6**

Tuesday 7

···· 07:50 ····

Wednesday 8

05:45

♒ 18:50

♊ **Thursday 9**

···· 08:50 ····

Friday 10

♋ **Saturday 11**

···· 19:50 ····

◑ 01:12 **Sunday 12**

♌ **Monday 13**

Perigee 21:52

☉♉ **Tuesday 14**

···· 07:50 ····

♍ **Wednesday 15**

Thursday 16

Descending moon

In a cold frame or nursery with good sun exposure (soil temperature should be higher than 11 °C/50 °F) sow celery (*Tall Utah, Ivory Tower*). Sow Swiss chard (*Bright Yellow, Lucullus*) in beds, digging furrows 40 cm (1 ½ ft) apart, watering the soil before seeding if it is dry. Disperse the seeds well, cover and water. Sow bulb fennel (*Florence, Orion*) in a sheltered nursery or under a tunnel. Sow slow-growing lettuce (*Craquerelle du Midi, Buttercrunch, Emerald Oak*).

Sow 3 seeds of melon or cucumber in holes of soil enriched with mature compost.

Sow salsify in the ground, spacing the seeds 20 cm (8 in) apart. Cover the seeds lightly, pack down and water. Thin when the plants have 2–3 leaves. Also sow chicory (*Zoom*), beets (*Moulin Rouge, Crapaudine, Kahira*) and carrots (*Flyaway, Maestro*).

On May 9, do not garden before 13:45
Plant the begonia semperflorens, pelargoniums and carnations sown on February 6–7. Plant the cauliflower and broccoli sown on March 5–6, spacing them 70 cm (just under 2 ½ ft) apart in all directions. Thin the annuals sown on April 2–3.

Under a tunnel, spaced 40 cm (1 ½ ft) apart, plant the chicory and curly endive sown on April 4–6. Plant herbs (basil, chervil, chives, tarragon, mint, sage, thyme) in pots or in the garden to repel parasites.

On May 13, do not garden before 16:45
Plant the aubergines, chilli peppers, sweet peppers and tomatoes sown on March 1–2, the physalis sown on March 11, the melons sown on April 7–8, and the courgette (zucchini), marrow and squash sown on April 23–25. Water and protect as required.

Lift the leeks sown on March 12–14 and leave them to dry for a day or two on the ground to fight off ringworm. Cut the roots to 2 cm (1 in) and the leaves to 10 cm (4 in), then plant them in the ground every 10 cm (4 in), burying the bases deeply. Thin the parsnips sown on April 9–10 to one plant every 20 cm (8 in), and the carrots and turnips sown on April 27–28 to one plant every 10 cm (4 in). Hoe and weed between each row.

Your notes and observations

August

August 2019

In UK/Ireland add 1 hour for BST

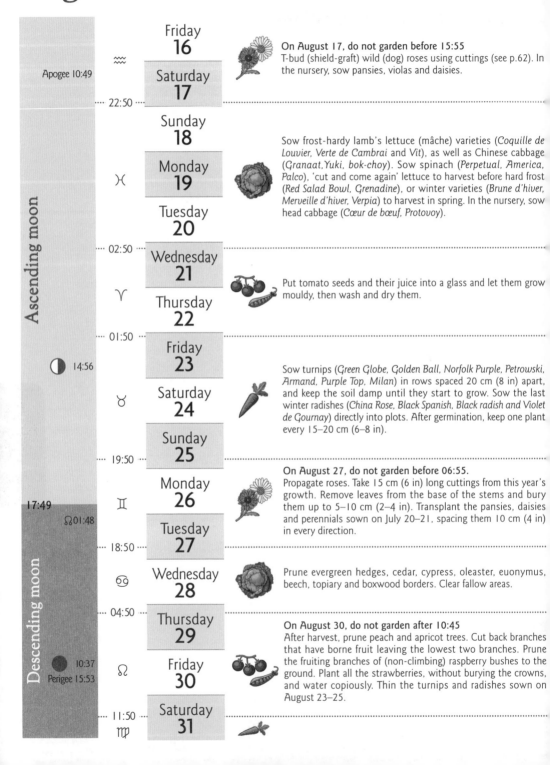

Ascending moon

Apogee 10:49

≈≈≈

Friday 16

Saturday 17

···· 22:50 ····

On August 17, do not garden before 15:55
T-bud (shield-graft) wild (dog) roses using cuttings (see p.62). In the nursery, sow pansies, violas and daisies.

Sunday 18

♓

Monday 19

Tuesday 20

Sow frost-hardy lamb's lettuce (mâche) varieties (*Coquille de Louvier, Verte de Cambrai* and *Vit*), as well as Chinese cabbage (*Granaat, Yuki,* bok-choy). Sow spinach (*Perpetual, America, Palco*), 'cut and come again' lettuce to harvest before hard frost (*Red Salad Bowl, Grenadine*), or winter varieties (*Brune d'hiver, Merveille d'hiver, Verpia*) to harvest in spring. In the nursery, sow head cabbage (*Cœur de bœuf, Protovoy*).

···· 02:50 ····

Wednesday 21

♈

Thursday 22

···· 01:50 ····

Put tomato seeds and their juice into a glass and let them grow mouldy, then wash and dry them.

◑ 14:56

Friday 23

♉

Saturday 24

Sunday 25

···· 19:50 ····

Sow turnips (*Green Globe, Golden Ball, Norfolk Purple, Petrowski, Armand, Purple Top, Milan*) in rows spaced 20 cm (8 in) apart, and keep the soil damp until they start to grow. Sow the last winter radishes (*China Rose, Black Spanish, Black radish* and *Violet de Gournay*) directly into plots. After germination, keep one plant every 15–20 cm (6–8 in).

17:49

Ω01:48

♊

Monday 26

Tuesday 27

···· 18:50 ····

On August 27, do not garden before 06:55.
Propagate roses. Take 15 cm (6 in) long cuttings from this year's growth. Remove leaves from the base of the stems and bury them up to 5–10 cm (2–4 in). Transplant the pansies, daisies and perennials sown on July 20–21, spacing them 10 cm (4 in) in every direction.

Descending moon

♋

Wednesday 28

Prune evergreen hedges, cedar, cypress, oleaster, euonymus, beech, topiary and boxwood borders. Clear fallow areas.

···· 04:50 ····

Thursday 29

● 10:37

Perigee 15:53

♌

Friday 30

On August 30, do not garden after 10:45
After harvest, prune peach and apricot trees. Cut back branches that have borne fruit leaving the lowest two branches. Prune the fruiting branches of (non-climbing) raspberry bushes to the ground. Plant all the strawberries, without burying the crowns, and water copiously. Thin the turnips and radishes sown on August 23–25.

···· 11:50 ····

♍

Saturday 31

Your notes and observations

August

September 2019

In UK/Ireland add 1 hour for BST

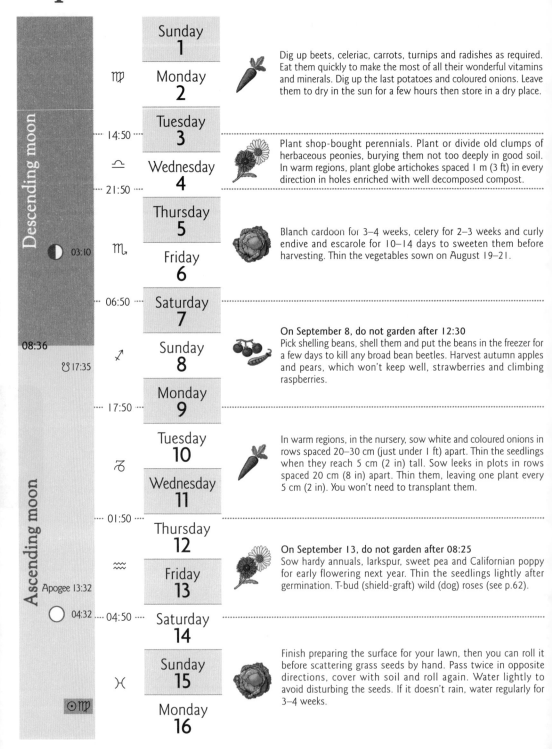

Descending moon

♍

14:50 Tuesday

♎

21:50

◑ 03:10 ♏

06:50

08:36

☊ 17:35 ♐

17:50

Ascending moon

♑

01:50

Apogee 13:32

○ 04:32 04:50 ♒

♓

⊙♍

	Sunday **1**
Monday **2**	
Tuesday **3**	
Wednesday **4**	
Thursday **5**	
Friday **6**	
Saturday **7**	
Sunday **8**	
Monday **9**	
Tuesday **10**	
Wednesday **11**	
Thursday **12**	
Friday **13**	
Saturday **14**	
Sunday **15**	
Monday **16**	

Dig up beets, celeriac, carrots, turnips and radishes as required. Eat them quickly to make the most of all their wonderful vitamins and minerals. Dig up the last potatoes and coloured onions. Leave them to dry in the sun for a few hours then store in a dry place.

Plant shop-bought perennials. Plant or divide old clumps of herbaceous peonies, burying them not too deeply in good soil. In warm regions, plant globe artichokes spaced 1 m (3 ft) in every direction in holes enriched with well decomposed compost.

Blanch cardoon for 3–4 weeks, celery for 2–3 weeks and curly endive and escarole for 10–14 days to sweeten them before harvesting. Thin the vegetables sown on August 19–21.

On September 8, do not garden after 12:30
Pick shelling beans, shell them and put the beans in the freezer for a few days to kill any broad bean beetles. Harvest autumn apples and pears, which won't keep well, strawberries and climbing raspberries.

In warm regions, in the nursery, sow white and coloured onions in rows spaced 20–30 cm (just under 1 ft) apart. Thin the seedlings when they reach 5 cm (2 in) tall. Sow leeks in plots in rows spaced 20 cm (8 in) apart. Thin them, leaving one plant every 5 cm (2 in). You won't need to transplant them.

On September 13, do not garden after 08:25
Sow hardy annuals, larkspur, sweet pea and Californian poppy for early flowering next year. Thin the seedlings lightly after germination. T-bud (shield-graft) wild (dog) roses (see p.62).

Finish preparing the surface for your lawn, then you can roll it before scattering grass seeds by hand. Pass twice in opposite directions, cover with soil and roll again. Water lightly to avoid disturbing the seeds. If it doesn't rain, water regularly for 3–4 weeks.

Your notes and observations

September

September 2019

In UK/Ireland add 1 hour for BST

Ascending moon

☉ ♍

♓

Monday 16

08:50

Tuesday 17

In the vegetable garden, sow green manure crops on empty plots, scattering the seeds by hand – white mustard, white turnip, vetch – to be buried next spring. Sow frost-hardy lamb's lettuce (mâche) and winter spinach in rows. Scatter the seeds well, cover, pack down with the back of a rake and water lightly.

♈

Wednesday 18

Thin tomato and grape vines to encourage them to ripen. Harvest seasonal fruits and fruit-vegetables.

07:50

Thursday 19

♉

Friday 20

Sow radishes (*Gaudry 2, 18-day, Flamboyant 5, National 2*) in a plot in rows spaced 20 cm (8 in) apart. Scatter the seeds well, cover, pack down and water lightly. Thin them a few days after they start to grow. If it doesn't rain, water regularly to prevent them from becoming too spicy.

Saturday 21

◑ 02:40 02:50

Sunday 22

01:51
Autumnal Equinox
☊ 06:29
07:50

♊

Monday 23

On September 23, do not garden before 11:35
Plant early-flowering spring bulbs – daffodil (narcissus), crocus, snowdrop – and the biennials sown on June 22–24 and July 20–21. In the nursery, transplant the pansies, violas and daisies sown on August 16–17.

04:50

Tuesday 24

♋

Descending moon

Wednesday 25

Propagate evergreen shrubs in a cold frame, and protect them over winter. In the nursery, transplant the head cabbages sown on August 19–21, spacing them 10 cm (4 in) apart.

15:50

Thursday 26

♌

Plant strawberries 30 cm (1 ft) apart in rows spaced 40 cm (1 ½ ft) apart. If they are bare-root plants, spread the roots out on little mounds and cover without burying the crowns. Plant shop bought soft-fruit plants. Place a flat stone under marrows and pumpkins to protect them from humidity and encourage them to ripen.

Friday 27

22:50

Perigree 02:23

● 18:26

Saturday 28

On September 28, do not garden before 07:30
Plant the onions sown on August 14–15. Move the strongest plants first and let the others grow a little longer. Trim the tips of the leaves and trim the roots to 1 cm (½ in) from the bulb. Plant them in a sunny plot in rows spaced 15 cm (6 in) apart, every 8 cm (3 in), burying the bulbs 3 cm (1 in) deep. Pack down but do not water.

♍

Sunday 29

Monday 30

Your notes and observations

October 2019

Descending moon

··· 00:50 ···
♎

Tuesday
1

Plant azalea, rhododendron and pieris in rich acid soils, covering the soil with compost.

··· 06:50 ···
Wednesday
2

♏

Thursday
3

Plant or divide lily of the valley in the semi-shade. Space the plants 10 cm (4 in) apart, barely burying the roots. Plant shop-bought conifers and evergreen shrubs so they can start to take root before the hard frost. Blanch curly endive, escarole, cardoon and celery.

··· 13:50 ···
Friday
4

15:15 ◐ 16:47
♉ 18:49
♐

Saturday
5

On October 5, do not garden after 13:40
In mild regions, sow round peas (*Petit Provençal, Douce Provence, Serpette Guilloteaux, Avalanche*) or mangetout (*Carouby de Maussane, Oregon sugar pod*). Hoe once they start to grow. To provide graft stock, layer peach, apricot and plum pits in a pot filled with sand and bury them at the foot of a north-facing wall so they remain dormant.

Sunday
6

··· 23:50 ···
Monday
7

♑

Under shelter, in well-refined soil, sow medium-long carrots (*Touchon, Nanco, Bolero*) for harvesting in April–May. Sift mature compost and spread it over vegetable plots or flowerbeds in a fine layer without digging it in. Feed the new compost heap with seasonal waste.

Tuesday
8

··· 08:50 ···
Wednesday
9

Ascending moon

Apogee 18:28

♒

Thursday
10

On October 10, do not garden after 13:20
Sow perennial sweet peas in front of a trellis or wire fence, adding sand to heavy soils. Plant 5 seeds in each hole, cover, pack down and water. Mark where you planted them, as they won't germinate until March–April 2020. Harvest saffron and leave it to dry.

··· 10:50 ···
Friday
11

Saturday
12

♓

Sow rows of winter spinach (*America, Palco, Monstrueux de Viroflay, Atlanta*), lamb's lettuce (mâche) (*Verte d'Étampes, Verte de Cambrai*) and winter lettuce (*Valdor, Winter Marvel, Rouge D'Hiver*). If necessary, place them under a tunnel. Sow green manure crops on empty plots, scattering the seeds by hand and raking to lightly bury them. Cut and bury them next spring.

Sunday
13

○ 21:07

Monday
14

··· 14:50 ···

Tuesday
15

♈

In mild regions, sow broad beans (fava). Harvest fruit and vegetable-fruits before the frost.

··· 13:50 ···
♉
Wednesday
16

Your notes and observations

October

October 2019

Ascending moon

♈ 13:50

Wednesday **16**

♉

Thursday **17**

Friday **18**

In a cold frame or tunnel, sow radishes (*French Breakfast, Gaudry 2, Sparkler*). Thin them after they start to grow for harvesting in 3–4 weeks. To aid germination, layer root chervil seeds in a container with sand. Cover with wire to protect from birds, and bury the pot at the foot of a north-facing wall, to sow in March 2020.

08:50

Saturday **19**

08:07 ☊07:28

♊

Sunday **20**

On October 20, do not garden before 12:35
Plant spring bulbs and lilies (except Madonna varieties). Protect globe artichokes by tying them loosely and earthing them up to 25 cm (10 in) high. Cover them with straw now or later on, depending on the local climate.

◑ 12:39 11:50

Monday **21**

♋

Tuesday **22**

Cut asparagus stems to soil level and burn the waste. Dig the plot and add compost. Plant the head cabbages sown on August 19–21, spacing them 40 cm (1 ½ ft) apart in every direction.

23:50

Wednesday **23**

♌

Thursday **24**

Plant strawberries and soft fruit shrubs 1 m (3 ft) apart, planting raspberries in front of a frame. Dig holes for fruit trees for planting in November–December. Pick rotten fruit and dead leaves and burn them. Treat any wounds with fungicide (or similar).

08:50

Friday **25**

Descending moon

Perigee 10:39

On October 26, do not garden.

Saturday **26**

♍

Sunday **27**

On October 26, do not garden.
Plant the onions sown on September 10–11. Gardeners in all areas can plant grey shallots (*Griselle*). Harvest and store any vegetables that will not last over winter, and protect those that will. Carefully dig up chicory without damaging the roots. Leave them to dry outside for a few days to stop growth. Thin the carrots sown on October 7–8.
On October 27, in UK/Ireland, clocks go back to GMT.

● 03:38 10:50

Monday **28**

♎

Tuesday **29**

Plant the pansies, violas and daisies sown on August 16–17. Plant any remaining shop-bought perennials and flowering shrubs. Dig up tuberous begonias, cannas, dahlias and gladiolas, and store them in a frost-free place.

16:50

Wednesday **30**

♏

Thursday **31**

Save the strongest endive plants. Trim the leaves to 3 cm (1 in) and the roots to 20 cm (8 in). Plant them in a ditch in the garden or a box in the basement. Surround them with earth, and water. Cover with straw or black plastic.

22:50

Your notes and observations

November 2019

Descending moon 00:33 ☊ 21:39

♐

Friday 1

On November 1, do not garden after 16:30
In mild regions, sow round, dwarf or climbing peas (*Petit Provençal, Douce Provence, Serpette Guilloteaux, Avalanche*) or mangetout (*Carouby de Maussane, Oregon sugar pod*).

Saturday 2

···· 07:50 ····

Sunday 3

◑ 10:23   ♑

Monday 4

Under a cold frame or tunnel, sow short bell carrots (*Parmex, Caracas*) and round radishes (*Gaudry 2, Amethyst*). Remove shoots from seed potatoes, inspect any stored vegetables and eat any that are starting to spoil.

Tuesday 5

···· 15:50 ····

Wednesday 6

♒

On November 7, do not garden before 13:40
Harvest broccoli and cauliflower as required. In mild regions, dead-head hydrangea stems that have finished flowering. Cut above the first bud beneath the flower. Finish pruning at the end of winter.

Apogee 08:36

Thursday 7

···· 17:50 ····

Ascending moon

Friday 8

♓

Harvest lamb's lettuce (mâche), spinach, head and 'cut and come again' lettuce, Chinese and Savoy cabbage, kale, cardoon, celery and fennel bulb. After the first frost, harvest winter varieties of Brussels sprouts, starting with those at the base of the stems. Cut tarragon to 10 cm (4 in) from the ground and cover with a good layer of dry leaves or straw.

Saturday 9

Sunday 10

···· 21:50 ····

Monday 11

♈

After the first frost, pick fruit such as medlars and persimmons (Sharon fruit). Eat them overripe. Press ripe olives.

○ 13:34

Tuesday 12

···· 19:50 ····

Wednesday 13

♉

Thursday 14

Make use of this quiet gardening period to take stock of your crops over the past year and note areas for improvement. Start planning your vegetable garden for 2020. Consider crop rotation and plant companionships (see p. 28–29). Identify any plots that shouldn't be fertilised.

Friday 15

···· 14:50 ····

♊ ☊ 08:48

13:53

Saturday 16

On November 16, do not garden before 13:55
Pull up tuberous begonias, dahlias (and divide them), cannas and gladiolas and store them in a dry place.

▶▶▶

Your notes and observations

November 2019

♌ 08:48
13:53

13:53

♊

Saturday
16

Sunday
17

···· 16:50 ····

♋

Monday
18

···· 05:50 ····

☉ ♏
21:10

Tuesday
19

♌

Wednesday
20

Thursday
21

···· 16:50 ····

Descending moon

Perigee 07:40

♍

Friday
22

Saturday
23

Sunday
24

···· 20:50 ····

♎

Monday
25

···· 02:50 ····

Tuesday
26

15:05

♏

Wednesday
27

···· 08:50 ····

Thursday
28

♉ 04:12
10:33

Ascending moon

♐

Friday
29

···· 16:50 ····
♑

Saturday
30

On November 16, do not garden before 13:55
Plant a clematis at the foot of a wall with a trellis or the foot of a tree. Place the roots in a hole and guide the shoots towards the support. Plant the last Hemerocallis (daylilies) and bare-root peonies.

Blanch endive, cardoon and celery. Clean dandelions and cover them with opaque pots for harvesting in 3–4 weeks.

Plant bare-root fruit trees when there is no frost, in soil well mixed with compost and horn meal. Plant stakes to support them, and make sure the grafting sites are above ground. Give each tree 1–2 watering cans full of water. When the fruit trees shed their leaves, spray them with fungicide (or similar). Prune fig tree branches. Earth up the beans sown on October 15–16.

On November 23, do not garden before 12:45
In mild regions, plant shallots (*Jermor, Longor, Mikor*) and grey shallots (*Griselle*). Space rows 25 cm (10 in) apart and the shallots 15 cm (6 in) apart, with the pointy tip barely buried. You can also plant white and purple garlic. Pull up Chinese artichokes, salsify, horseradish, Jerusalem artichokes, parsnips and leeks as required. Spread a layer of straw over the soil to protect crops from the frost and continue your harvest. Dig heavy soil without damaging roots.

Prune rose shrubs and treat with fungicide (or similar). Cut back dried growth on perennials. Crush and compost the waste if it's healthy. Don't cut back grass or non-hardy plants.

Force endives either in the garden or in a dark room (see p.21). Finish planting head cabbages. Plant hedges of privet, hornbeam and beech, and climbing plants such as ivy and creepers, in front of walls.

On November 29, do not garden before 09:20
In mild regions, sow beans and peas. In warm regions, harvest the remaining olives and take them for pressing. Layer apple and pear pips in pots with sand for future rootstock.

Your notes and observations

November

December 2019

Ascending moon

Day	Moon info
Sunday **1**	♑
Monday **2**	... 23:50 ...

Remove long shoots from seed potatoes to prevent loss of reserves. Inspect vegetables in storage and throw away any that are rotting to avoid contaminating the others. Clean tools, sand wooden handles and oil them. Sharpen and grease spade blades.

Day	Moon info
Tuesday **3**	☽ 06:58 ≈≈≈
Wednesday **4**	Apogee 04:08 ... 01:50 ...

On December 5, do not garden before 09:15
In the house, treat flowering plants such as azaleas and cyclamens. Bathe them in luke-warm, non-calcareous water. Let them dry and replace. In a warm greenhouse, sow begonia semperflorens and pelargoniums in pots.

Day	Moon info
Thursday **5**	
Friday **6**	♓
Saturday **7**	... 05:50 ...

Harvest Brussels sprouts, lamb's lettuce (mâche), spinach and lettuce. Protect fragile crops with a fleece or tunnel. In little dishes, sprout lentils, chickpeas and soybeans. Their young shoots are packed with vitamins and minerals. In a warm spot in the house, sow a few orange, lemon or grapefruit pips in pots. They will grow into pretty, green, exotic-looking plants, but they will not produce fruit.

Day	Moon info
Sunday **8**	♈
Monday **9**	... 03:50 ...

In mild regions, sow round peas and mangetout.

Day	Moon info
Tuesday **10**	♉
Wednesday **11**	○ 05:12
Thursday **12**	... 21:50 ...

Sow round radishes (*Gaudry 2, Cherriette*) and short carrots under a frame. Thin them, keeping one plant every 5 cm (2 in). Air them when the weather is mild. Inspect vegetables in storage and throw away any that are rotting to avoid contaminating the others. When you have decided on your plan for next year's garden, determine which seeds you need and buy them.

Day	Moon info
Friday **13**	♊ ☊ 14:14 **20:58**
Saturday **14**	... 22:50 ...

On December 13, do not garden after 09:10
If it's not freezing, plant roses and bare-root flowering shrubs. Ensure the grafting sites of roses are at soil level, not below. Take cuttings from wild (dog) roses for grafting next summer. Force more endives, in the garden or in a box in a dark room, packing them with earth or straw and covering with black plastic.

Descending moon

Day	Moon info
Sunday **15**	♋
Monday **16**	... 10:50 ... ♌

Pull up and replant raspberry shoots.

Your notes and observations

December 2019

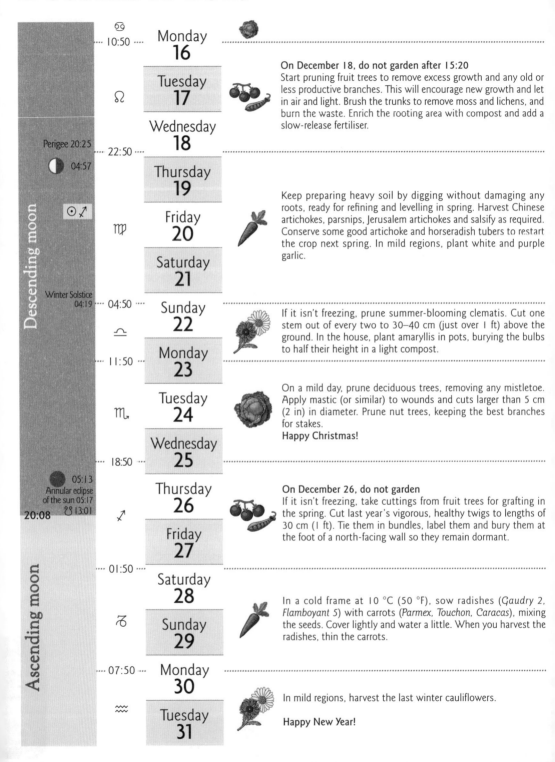

Descending moon

Perigee 20:25
04:57
⊙ ♐
Winter Solstice 04:19
Annular eclipse of the sun 05:17
05:13
♉ 13:01
20:08

Ascending moon

♋ 10:50 — Monday **16**

♌ — Tuesday **17**

22:50 — Wednesday **18**

— Thursday **19**

♍ — Friday **20**

— Saturday **21**

04:50 — Sunday **22**

♎ — 11:50 — Monday **23**

♏ — Tuesday **24**

18:50 — Wednesday **25**

♐ — Thursday **26**

— Friday **27**

01:50 — Saturday **28**

♑ — Sunday **29**

07:50 — Monday **30**

♒ — Tuesday **31**

On December 18, do not garden after 15:20
Start pruning fruit trees to remove excess growth and any old or less productive branches. This will encourage new growth and let in air and light. Brush the trunks to remove moss and lichens, and burn the waste. Enrich the rooting area with compost and add a slow-release fertiliser.

Keep preparing heavy soil by digging without damaging any roots, ready for refining and levelling in spring. Harvest Chinese artichokes, parsnips, Jerusalem artichokes and salsify as required. Conserve some good artichoke and horseradish tubers to restart the crop next spring. In mild regions, plant white and purple garlic.

If it isn't freezing, prune summer-blooming clematis. Cut one stem out of every two to 30–40 cm (just over 1 ft) above the ground. In the house, plant amaryllis in pots, burying the bulbs to half their height in a light compost.

On a mild day, prune deciduous trees, removing any mistletoe. Apply mastic (or similar) to wounds and cuts larger than 5 cm (2 in) in diameter. Prune nut trees, keeping the best branches for stakes.
Happy Christmas!

On December 26, do not garden
If it isn't freezing, take cuttings from fruit trees for grafting in the spring. Cut last year's vigorous, healthy twigs to lengths of 30 cm (1 ft). Tie them in bundles, label them and bury them at the foot of a north-facing wall so they remain dormant.

In a cold frame at 10 °C (50 °F), sow radishes (*Gaudry 2, Flamboyant 5*) with carrots (*Parmex, Touchon, Caracas*), mixing the seeds. Cover lightly and water a little. When you harvest the radishes, thin the carrots.

In mild regions, harvest the last winter cauliflowers.

Happy New Year!

Your notes and observations

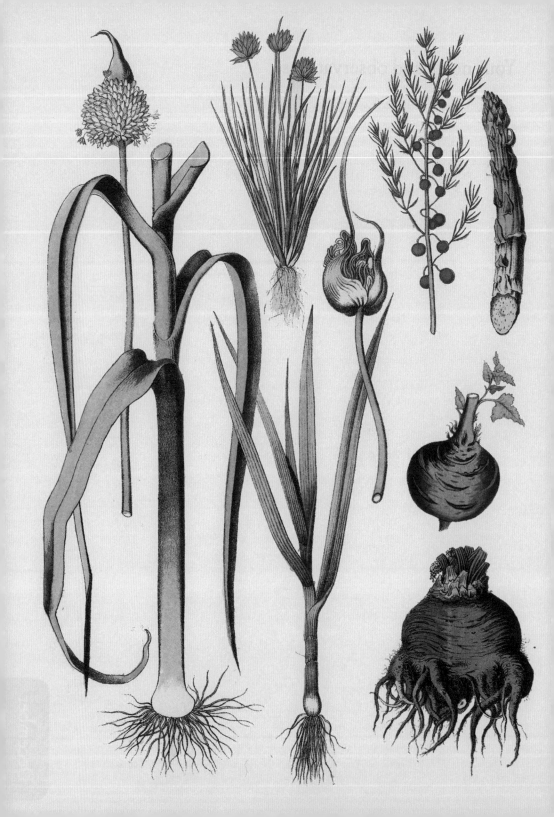

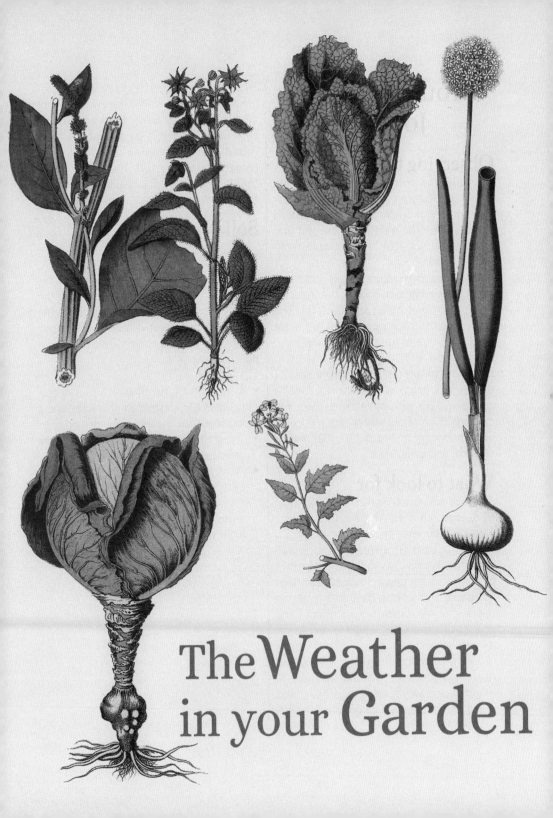

The Weather
in your Garden

Your Weather Journal

Observing the weather

You will often notice differences between the weather forecast and the actual weather in your garden. There are several ways to better predict the weather where you live, but here we will look at the simplest and most natural.

It also helps to record details about the weather in a logbook and on the monthly charts provided here (pp. 92–103). The more specific your notes are, the more accurate your predictions will become. In turn, you will take greater pleasure in observing nature and the movements of the sky. A logbook is a very useful tool for recording your gardening experience. You can carry it over from year to year, enriching your knowledge and easing the planning of seasonal and daily tasks.

What to look for

Altitude and other features of the local landscape can affect the weather in your garden: there may be a hill or mountain nearby, or perhaps a tree, hedge or wall protects you from the wind. The reverse may be true: a valley might channel important air currents, or a nearby lake may create an updraught. Microclimates are infinite and your garden is unique, which means so are its weather patterns.

Will it be warm and sunny? Will it rain? It can help to look at the sky for clues. A bright moon surrounded by a halo, or a veiled sun in the evening often mean rain.

Through observation, you can learn which wind drives away clouds, clears the sky or allows the Sun to shine. Birds and insects can 'smell' the rain or an approaching thunderstorm, behaving in ways we can recognise and use too. The shape of the clouds can also help; consult an illustrated book on clouds for reference.

Soli-lunar charts

How to use them

The soli-lunar charts shown here are graduated in 5° bands with 0° marking the equator. Positive declinations are above the equator line and negative declinations below. If you are in the Southern hemisphere, turn the chart upside down.

- Dates of the lunar phases, Moon nodes, perigees and apogees are all marked and a key to symbols used is provided on p.36
- The path of the Sun is marked in dark green, and the Moon in light green
- As in the example on p.90, make notes every day, for example the colour of the sky, any rain, sun, clear weather, variable wind, the lowest night temperature, highest daytime temperature, etc.

The Sun

On January 1 at midnight (00:00), the declination[1] of the Sun is −23°03′ (see chart p. 92). The Sun is gaining height from its lowest point at the winter solstice.

At the time of the spring equinox, the curve of the Sun intersects with the equator and day and night are the same duration. The Sun's declination becomes positive, temperatures gradually climb, sap rises in plants and flowers start to bloom.

The Sun reaches its highest point (+23°26′) at the time of the summer solstice on June 21, before starting its descent, crossing the equator again at the time of the autumn equinox (p. 100) and falling to its lowest level at the winter solstice (23°26′, p. 103).

The constant pace of the Sun, identical every year, regulates the length of our days, and the rise and fall of plants' sap.

The Moon

The Moon's movement changes from one year to the next in relation to the Earth, the Sun and the ecliptic, thus causing many variations.

In 2019, the Moon is descending for the first few days of the year, arriving at its lowest lunistice[2] when in Sagittarius, on January 5 at 17:42. It then ascends, to reach its highest lunistice on January 19 at 23:18, in Gemini.

_____

1 Declination: distance of a star from the plane of the celestial equator (horizontal line 0° on the charts).
2 Lunistice: time when the Moon reaches the farthest distance north or south of the celestial equator.

There are 13 days, 15 hours, 15 minutes and 30 seconds between two lunistices and the crossings of the equator, the complete cycle of the sidereal revolution being 27 days, 7 hours, 43 minutes and 11 seconds.

Changes in weather usually occur at the time of lunistices, especially on the third day.

Let's take an example in April

Note carefully the weather on April 12, 13, and 14 in particular.

- If the weather is fair and the wind blows from the direction of the good weather, it should last until the full moon on the 19th.
- If the weather is variable on the 14th, changeable with cloudy skies and rain showers, you can expect sunny intervals ahead. Note that on the day the Moon crosses the equator (18th) there may be some small changes.

Remember, when it comes to weather forecasting, no system is infallible. Hopefully, this method will help you to plan your gardening tasks in some way.

Soli-lunar Charts

How to use the charts: an example

Each monthly chart allows you to note the main weather variations each day.

Day	Rain (mm) daily	Rain (mm) month to date	Temp (°C) min	Temp (°C) max	Wind	Air pressure	Weather features
31 Tue			5	10	SE		Fair sunny intervals, mild
30 Mon	3	62	4	7		1042	Overcast, drizzle, mild
29 Sun			−2	7		1045	Fog, rain, sunny intervals
28 Sat	10	59	2	6		1040	Light showers, fog in the evening
27 Fri			5	3	SE	1036	Cloudy
26 Thu			−6	2	SE	1036	Overcast, wind gusts in the evening
25 Wed			−8	4		1042	Sunny intervals
24 Tue			−8	4	N	1043	Fair
23 Mon Ap.			−3	6		1042	Fair to cloudy
22 Sun			−4	7		1044	Overcast
21 Sat			−6	8		1045	Fair
20 Fri			−7	3		1046	Fair
19 Thu			−11	3		1046	Fair, milder
18 Wed			−11	−1		1045	Sunny, cold
17 Tue			−7	1	NE	1041	Fair, cold
16 Mon	2	49	−2	2	N	1042	Some snow in the morning, sunny intervals
15 Sun	3	47	−3	1		1043	Snow in the morning, some sun
14 Sat	22	44	−4	1		1042	Snow turning to rain
13 Fri	4	22	−1	5		1039	Snow early and for the rest of the day
12 Thu	5	18	2	6		1032	Fog, rain
11 Wed	13		−2	5		1045	Fog, rain
10 Tue Per.			1	5	NO	1036	Fog, overcast
9 Mon			−6	3		1044	Sunny intervals
8 Sun			−4	4		1050	Fair
7 Sat			−7	5		1051	Fair
6 Fri			−8	1		1053	Fair, some clouds
5 Thu			−4	3	NO	1051	Fair
4 Wed			−8	2		1045	Fair, milder
3 Tue			−6	3	NO	1047	Fair, then cold
2 Mon			−5	5		1045	Sunny intervals, light clouds
1 Sun			−3	5		1044	Fair

This example was noted in January 2017. The third day after the lunistice, January 13 and 27 provide important indications for the 10 days following.

+30° +25° +20° +15° +10° +5° 0° −5° −10° −15° −20° −25° −30°

In dark green, the passage of the Sun in front of Sagittarius and Capricorn. In light green, the curve and passage of the Moon in front of the constellations.

This chart allows you to visualise the large curve of the Sun, the small monthly curves of the Moon, their ascending movement (times for sowing) and descending movement (times for preparing the earth, transplanting and planting).

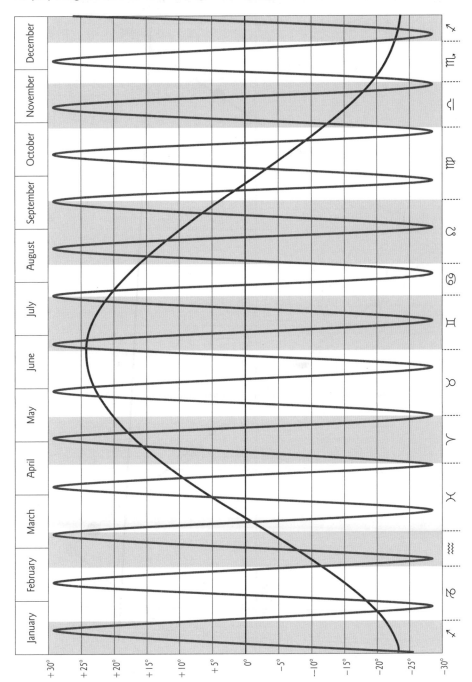

January 2019

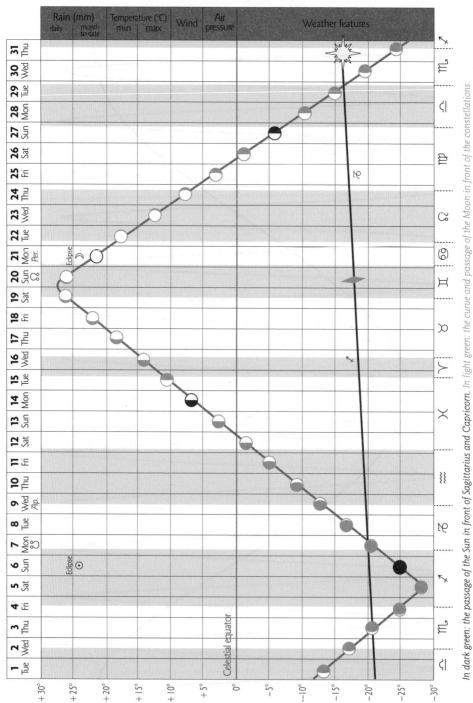

In dark green: the passage of the Sun in front of Sagittarius and Capricorn. In light green: the curve and passage of the Moon in front of the constellations.

February 2019

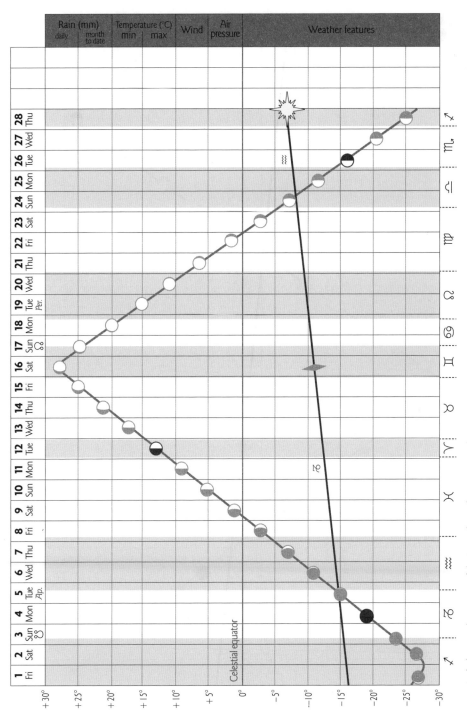

	Rain (mm)		Temperature (°C)		Wind	Air pressure	Weather features
	daily	month to date	min	max			

In dark green: the passage of the Sun in front of Capricorn and Aquarius. In light green: the curve and passage of the Moon in front of the constellations.

March 2019

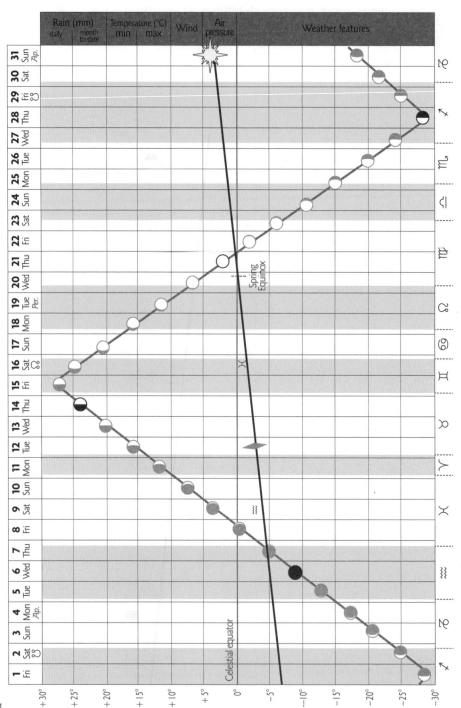

In dark green: the passage of the Sun in front of Aquarius and Pisces. In light green: the curve and passage of the Moon in front of the constellations.

April 2019

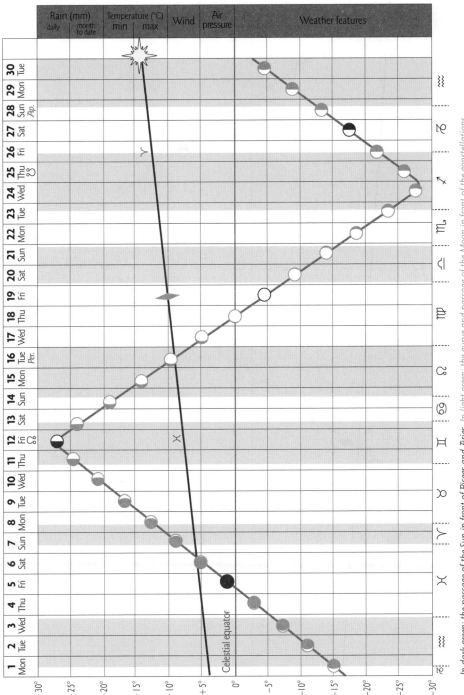

In dark green: the passage of the Sun in front of Pisces and Aries. In light green: the curve and passage of the Moon in front of the constellations.

May 2019

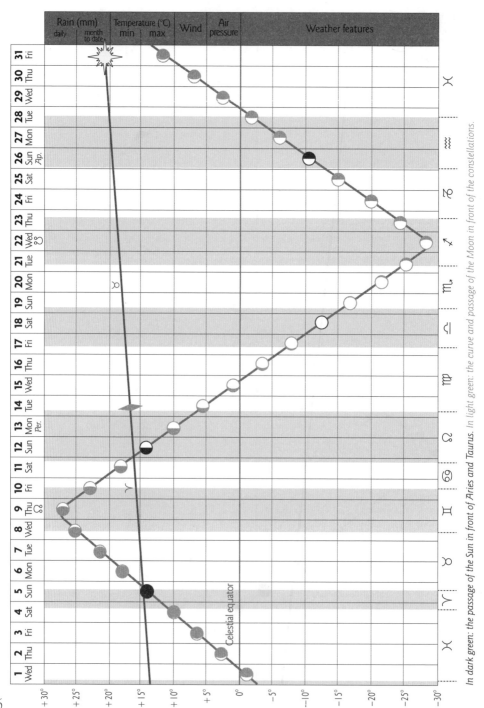

In dark green: the passage of the Sun in front of Aries and Taurus. In light green: the curve and passage of the Moon in front of the constellations.

June 2019

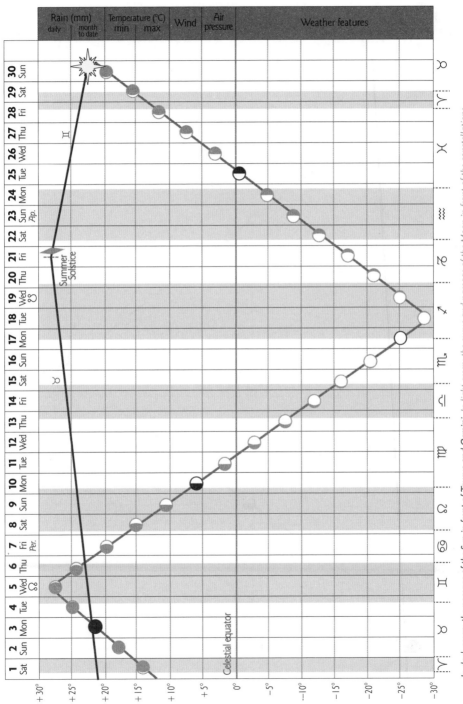

In dark green: the passage of the Sun in front of Taurus and Gemini. In light green: the curve and passage of the Moon in front of the constellations.

July 2019

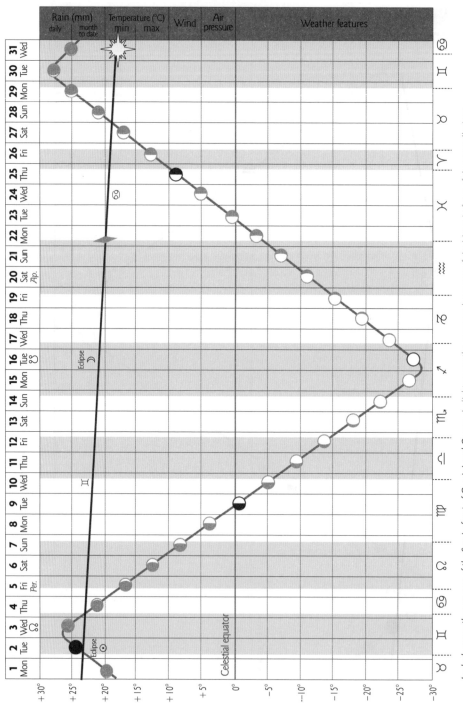

In dark green: the passage of the Sun in front of Gemini and Cancer. In light green: the curve and passage of the Moon in front of the constellations.

August 2019

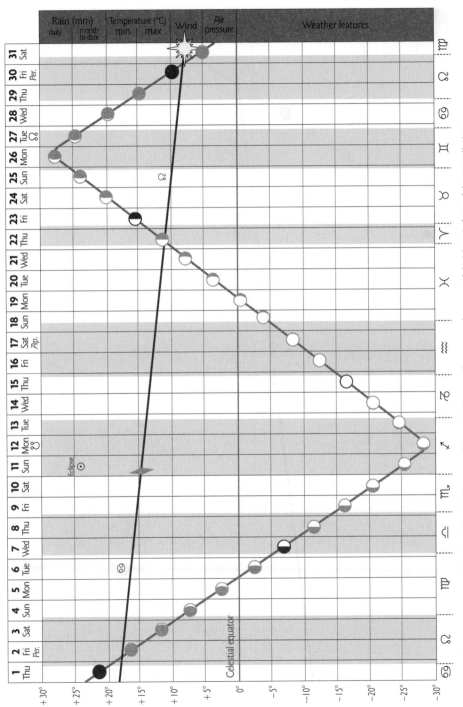

In dark green: the passage of the Sun in front of Cancer and Leo. In light green: the curve and passage of the Moon in front of the constellations.

September 2019

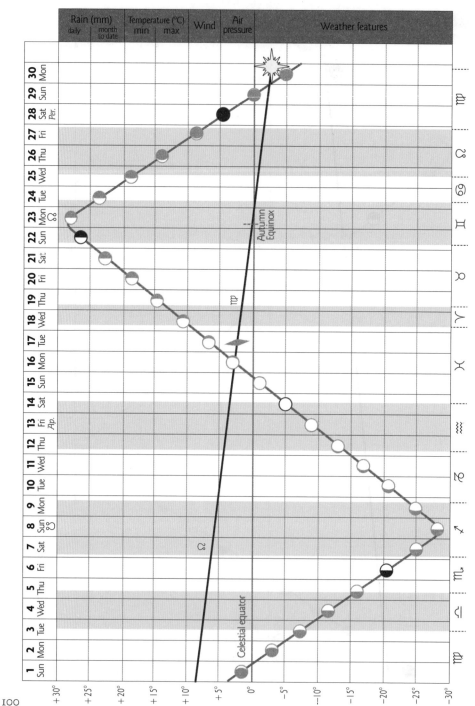

In dark green: the passage of the Sun in front of Leo and Virgo. In light green: the curve and passage of the Moon in front of the constellations.

October 2019

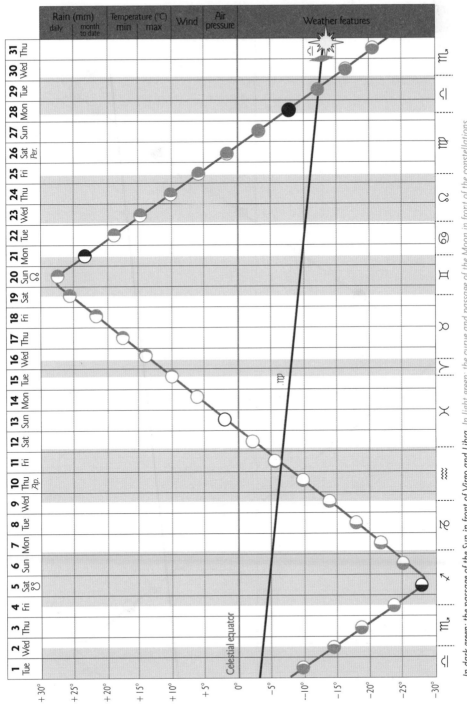

In dark green: the passage of the Sun in front of Virgo and Libra. In light green: the curve and passage of the Moon in front of the constellations.

November 2019

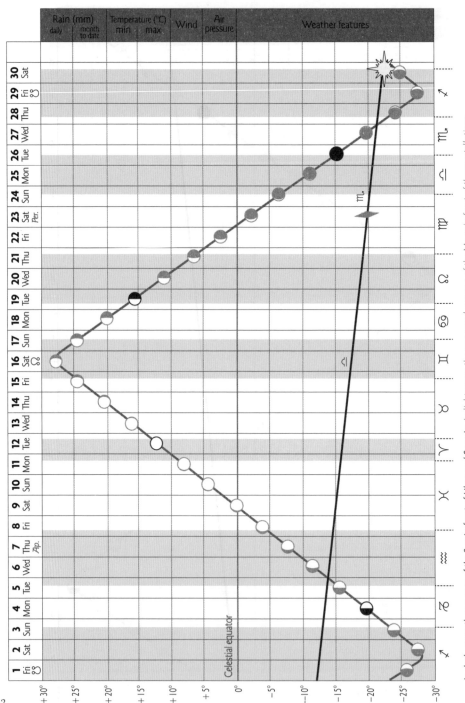

| | Rain (mm) | | Temperature (°C) | | Wind | Air pressure | Weather features |
| | daily | month to date | min | max | | | |

December 2019

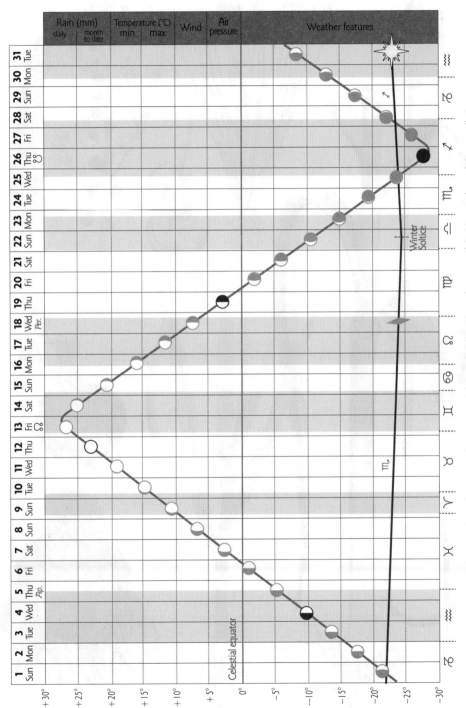

In dark green: the passage of the Sun in front of Scorpio and Sagittarius. In light green: the curve and passage of the Moon in front of the constellations.

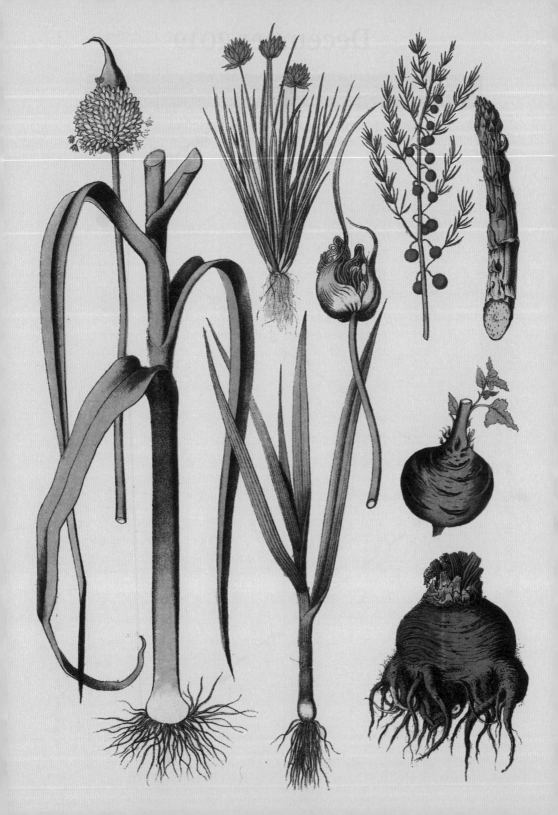

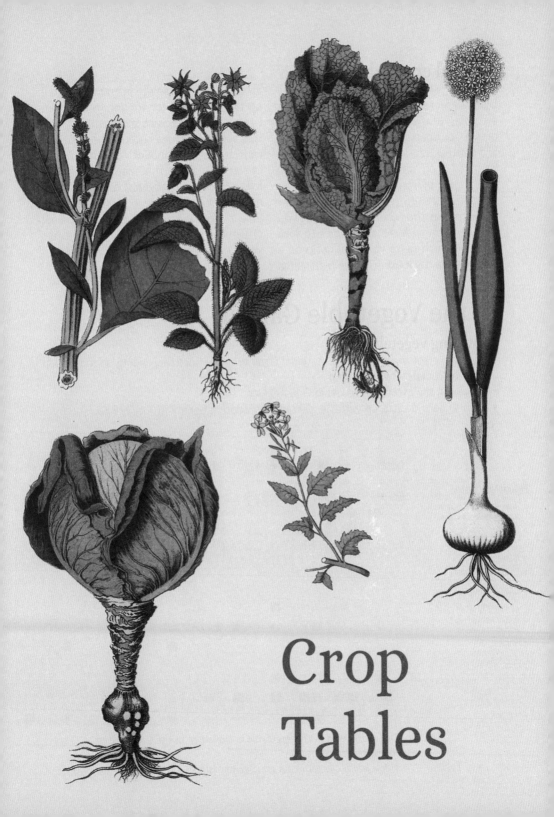

Crop
Tables

Annual crop tables

These annual crop tables will give you the best dates for sowing, planting and pruning according to the Moon. It is up to you to decide your personal gardening methods, and whether to grow your crops somewhere sheltered or on open ground, depending on the climate of your garden. The calendar pages (pp. 38–85) give all the necessary details about the Moon's cycles, but you can use them with the crop tables to keep track of which tasks you should do on a particular day by looking for the highlighted dates. Suggested soil temperatures stated on the tables are for sowing in the open earth (unless otherwise specified), but note that soil temperatures need to be higher for early seeding in containers. As mentioned earlier, it may be that you can't always follow our indicated harvest dates. On these days, we would suggest you make use of time indoors and do some garden planning, or perhaps make preserves with any crops you have already grown and harvested.

In the Vegetable Garden

Flowering vegetables

- Sow and plant in the greenhouse, under cover or in the open, depending on the season and the climate of your garden
- Sow with the ascendant Moon in Aquarius ≈≈
- Plant, hoe and earth up with the descending Moon in Gemini ♊ or Libra ♎

	Jan	Feb	Mar	Apr	May	Jun	Jul	Aug	Sep	Oct	Nov	Dec
Artichoke (globe)												
→ Remove cover. Keep two suckers from each stem		16/24	16/24	12/20				7/27	4/23			
→ Plant			16/24	12/20				7/27	4/23	1/21/29		
→ Water, fertilise, hoe			16/24	12/20	18	6/14	3/11/31	7/27	4/23			
→ Harvest					27	24	20	16	12			
→ Tie down, cover										1/21/29	17/25	14/22
Broccoli												
→ Sow (soil at 15 °C/60 °F*)			5	2/29	27	24	20					
→ Water lightly, transplant, hoe			16/24	12/20	18	6/14	3/11/31	7/27	4/23	1/21/29		
→ Harvest						24	20	16	12	11	6	
Cauliflower												
→ Sow (soil at 15 °C/60 °F*)	10	6	5	2/29	27	24						
→ Water regularly, transplant, hoe		16/24	16/24	12/20	18	6/14	3/11/31	7/27	4/23	1/21/29		
→ Harvest			5	2/29	27	24	20	16	12	11	6	3/31

The cultivation of the vegetable is explained in the Calendar on the highlighted date.

106 Crop Tables

*Ideal soil temperature for good germination.

Leafy vegetables

- Sow and plant in the greenhouse, under cover or in the open depending on the season and the climate of your garden
- Sow with the ascendant Moon in Pisces ♓
- Plant, hoe and earth up with the descending Moon in Cancer ♋ or Scorpio ♏

	Jan	Feb	Mar	Apr	May	Jun	Jul	Aug	Sep	Oct	Nov	Dec
Asparagus												
→ Prepare and enrich the soil	3/30	18/26								3/22/30	18/27	
→ Plant 1–2 year-old crowns			17/26	13/22								
→ Hoe, earth up			17/26	13/22								
→ Harvest the older plants				4	2.29							
→ Cut back, burn, add compost										3/22/30	18/27	
Cardoon												
→ Prepare and enrich the soil			17/26	13/22						3/22/30	18/27	
→ Sow (soil at 10 °C/50 °F*)					2/29							
→ Thin plants, hoe, water					20	7/16	4/13/31	1/9/28	6/24			
→ Earth up, blanch								1/9/28	6/24	3/22/30	18/27	
→ Harvest									15	12	9	6
Celery												
→ Prepare and enrich the soil		18/26	17/26									
→ Sow (soil at 12 °C/53 °F*)			8	4	2/29							
→ Transplant, plant, hoe				13/22	11/20	7/16	4/13/31	1/9/28	6/24			
→ Earth up, blanch							4/13/31	1/9/28	6/24	3/22/30	18/27	
→ Harvest								19	15	12	9	6
Chicory (witloof/Belgian endive)												
→ Transplant, force, blanch	3/30	18/26								3/22/30	18/27	15/24
Fennel												
→ Prepare and enrich the soil			17/26									
→ Sow (soil at 12 °C/53 °F*)				4	2/29	25	23	19				
→ Thin out, plant, earth up					11/20	7/16	4/13/31	1/9/28	6/24	3/22/30		
→ Harvest							23	19	15	12	9	6
Spinach												
→ Prepare and enrich the soil	3/30	18/26					4/13/31	1/9/28	6/24	3/22/30	18/27	
→ Sow (soil at 12 °C/53 °F*)		9	8	4				19	15	12		
→ Thin out, hoe			17/26	13/22	11/20			28	6/24	3/22/30	18/27	
→ Harvest	12	9	8	4	2/29					12	9	6
Swiss chard												
→ Prepare and enrich the soil			17/26							3/22/30	18/27	
→ Sow (soil at 10 °C/50 °F*)				4	2/29	25						
→ Thin, hoe					11/20	7/16	4/13/31	1/9/28	6/24	3/22/30		
→ Harvest			8	4	2/29		23	19	15	12	9	

The cultivation of the vegetable is explained in the Calendar on the highlighted date.

*Ideal soil temperature for good germination.

Year-round cabbages

- Sow and plant in the greenhouse, under cover or in the open depending on the season and the climate of your garden
- Sow with the ascendant Moon in Pisces ♓
- Plant, hoe and earth up with the descending Moon in Cancer ♋ or Scorpio ♏

	Jan	Feb	Mar	Apr	May	Jun	Jul	Aug	Sep	Oct	Nov	Dec
Brussels sprouts												
Prepare and enrich soil		18/26	17/26	13/22						3/22/30	18/27	
Sow in nursery			8	4	2/29							
Transplant in nursery, maintain			26	13/22	11/20	7/16						
Plant, maintain				13/22	11/20	7/16	4/13/31	1/9/28	6/24	3/22/30		
Harvest	12	9	8						15	12	9	6
Chinese cabbage												
Prepare and enrich soil				13/22	11/20	7/16						
Sow in plot						25	23	19	15			
Thin, maintain							4/13/31	1/9/28	6/24	3/22/30	18/27	
Harvest									15	12	9	6
Head cabbage												
Prepare and enrich soil		18/26	17/26	13/22						3/22/30	18/27	
Sow in warm conditions	12	9	8	4	2/29			19	15			
Transplant in nursery		18/26	17/26	13/22	11/20	7/16			6/24	3/22/30		
Plant, maintain			17/26	13/22	11/20	7/16	4/13/31	1/9/28	6/24	3/22/30	18/27	
Harvest					2/29	25	23	19	15	12	9	6
Kale										/		
Prepare and enrich soil		18/26	17/26	13/22						3/22/30	18/27	
Sow in nursery				4	2/29	25						
Transplant in nursery, maintain				22	11/20	7/16	4/13/31					
Plant, maintain					11/20	7/16	4/13/31	1/9/28	6/24	3/22/30	18/27	
Harvest	12	9	8							12	9	6
Savoy cabbage												
Prepare and enrich soil		18/26	17/26	13/22						3/22/30	18/27	
Sow in nursery			8	4	2/29	25						
Transplant in nursery, maintain			26	13/22	11/20	7/16	4/13/31					
Plant, maintain				22	11/20	7/16	4/13/31	1/9/28	6/24	3/22/30	18/27	
Harvest	12	9	8						15	12	9	6

The cultivation of the vegetable is explained in the Calendar on the highlighted date.

Year-round salad leaves

- Sow and plant in the greenhouse, under cover or in the open depending on the season and the climate of your garden
- Sow with the ascending Moon in Pisces ♓
- Plant, hoe and earth up with the descending Moon in Cancer ♋ or Scorpio ♏

	Jan	Feb	Mar	Apr	May	Jun	Jul	Aug	Sep	Oct	Nov	Dec
Cress												
Sow	12	9	8	4	2/29	25	23	19	15	12	9	6
Sow			8	4	2/29	25						
Dandelion												
Sow		9	8	4	2/29	25						
Pull out, plant				13/22	11/20	7/16	4/13/31	1/9/28				
Endive (chicory)												
Curly endive												
Sow			8	4	2/29	25	23					
Transplant, plant, maintain				13/22	11/20	7/16	4/13/31	1/9/28	6/24	3/22/30	18/27	
Escarole												
Sow			8	4	2/29	25	23					
Transplant, plant, maintain				13/22	11/20	7/16	4/13/31	1/9/28	6/24	3/22/30	18/27	
Radicchio												
Sow					2/29	25						
Thin out, maintain							7/16	4/13/31	1/9/28	6/24	3/22/30	
Wild chicory												
Sow					2/29	25						
Thin out, maintain							7/16	4/13/31	1/9/28	6/24	3/22/30	
Lettuce												
Batavia												
Sow	12	9	8	4	2/29	25	23	19	15			
Transplant, plant, maintain		18/26	17/26	13/22	11/20	7/16	4/13/31	1/9/28	6/24	3/22/30	18/27	
'Cut and come again' lettuce												
Sow	12	9	8	4	2/29	25	23	19	15			
Transplant, plant, maintain		18/26	17/26	13/22	11/20	7/16	4/13/31	1/9/28	6/24	3/22/30	18/27	
Head lettuce												
Sow	12	9	8	4	2/29	25	23	19				
Transplant, plant, maintain	30	18/26	17/26	13/22	11/20	7/16	4/13/31	1/9/28	6/24			
Lamb's lettuce (mâche)												
Sow							23	19	15	12		
Romaine												
Sow		9	8	4	2/29	25	23	19				
Transplant, plant, maintain			17/26	13/22	11/20	7/16	4/13/31	1/9/28	6/24			
Winter lettuce												
Sow								19	15	12		
Transplant, plant, maintain	3/30	18/26	17/26	13/22	11/20				6/24	3/22/30	18/27	15/24
Purslane												
Sow	12	9	8	4	2/29	25	23	19				
Rocket (arugula)												
Sow		9	8	4	2/29	25	23	19	15			

The cultivation of the vegetable is explained in the Calendar on the highlighted date.

Aromatic herbs

- Sow and plant in the greenhouse, under cover or in the open depending on the season and the climate of your garden
- Sow with the ascending Moon in Pisces ♓
- Plant, divide and prune with the descending Moon in Cancer ♋ or Scorpio ♏

		Jan	Feb	Mar	Apr	May	Jun	Jul	Aug	Sep	Oct	Nov	Dec
Annuals													
Basil	Sow in sheltered location			8	4								
	Plant				13/22	11/20							
Chervil	Sow in sheltered location	12	9									12	
	Sow in the sun			8	4					15			
	Sow in the shade					2/29	25	23	19				
	Thin, remove flowers		18/26	17/26	13/22	11/20	7/16	4/13/31	1/9/28	6/24	3/22/30	18/27	
Coriander (cilantro)	Sow				4	2/29	25			15			
Dill	Sow lightly				4	2/29	25						
Marjoram	Sow			8	4	2/29				15			
Parsley	Sow		9	8	4	2/29	25	23	19				
	Thin, remove flowers			17/26	13/22	11/20	7/16	4/16/31	1/9/28	6/24			
Perrenials													
Bay (laurel)	Plant, prune			17/26	13/22	11/20				6/24	3/22/30		
	Take cuttings								1/9/28	6/24	3/22/30		
Chive	Sow			8	4								
	Thin, transplant				13/22	11/20							
	Plant, divide			17/26	13/22	11/20				6/24	3/22/30		
Lemon-balm	Sow					2/29	25						
	Plant, divide			17/26	13/22	11/20				6/24	3/22/30		
Mint	Plant, divide			17/26	13/22	11/20							
	Cut back						7/16	4/13/31			3/22/30	18/27	
Oregano	Sow			8	4	2/29				15			
	Plant, divide			17/26	13/22	11/20				6/24	3/22/30		
Rosemary	Plant			17/26	13/22	11/20							
	Take cuttings				13/22	11/20			1/9/28	6/24			
Sage	Plant, prune			17/26	13/22	11/20							
	Take cuttings					11/20			1/9/28	6/24			
Savory	Plant			17/26	13/22	11/20				6/24			
	Take cuttings								1/9/28	6/24			
Sorrel	Sow		9	8	4	2/29	25						
	Plant, divide		18/26	17/26	13/22						3/22/30	18/27	
Tarragon	Plant, divide			17/26	13/22	11/20							
	Cut back, protect										3/22/30	18/27	
Thyme	Sow				4	2/29							
	Plant, divide				13/22	11/20				6/24	3/22/30		
	Prune						7/16	4/13/31	1/9/28				

The cultivation of the vegetable is explained in the Calendar on the highlighted date.

Root vegetables

- Sow and plant in the greenhouse, under cover or in the open depending on the season and the climate of your garden
- Sow with the ascendant Moon in Taurus ♉ or Capricorn ♑
- Do all other garden work with the descending Moon in Virgo ♍

Crop	Activity	Jan	Feb	Mar	Apr	May	Jun	Jul	Aug	Sep	Oct	Nov	Dec
et(root)	→ Sow (soil at 10 °C/50 °F*)			30	9/27	6/24	2/20/30						
	→ Thin, hoe				17	15	11	8	4/31	1/29	27		
	→ Harvest							8	4/31	1/29	27	22	
rrot	→ Sow (soil at 10 °C/50 °F*)	8/17	4/13	3/12/30	9/27	6/24	2/20/30	1/18/27	14/23	10/20	7/17	4/13	1/10/28
	→ Weed, thin	25	21	21	17	15	11	8	4/31	1/29	27	22	19
	→ Harvest				17	15	11	8	4/31	1/29	27	22	19
eriac	→ Sow (soil at 12 °C/53 °F*)		4/13	3/12/30	9/27	6/24							
	→ Transplant twice, plant				17	15	11						
	→ Harvest								4/31	1/29	27	22	
cory tloof/ jan endive)	→ Sow (soil at 14 °C/57 °F*)					6/24	2/20/30						
	→ Thin, weed						11	8	4/31	1/29	27		
	→ Pull out, then replant**										27		
inese ichoke	→ Plant		21	21	17								
	→ Hoe, weed			21	17	15	11	8	4/31	1/29	27		
	→ Harvest	25	21	21							27	22	19
rlic	→ Plant, hoe	25	21	21							27	22	19
	→ Harvest					15	11	8	4/31				
ek	→ Sow (soil at 10 °C/50 °F*)	8/17	4/13	3/12/30	9/27	6/24			14/23	10/20			
	→ Thin, plant, hoe		21	21	17	15	11	8	4/31	1/29	27	22	
	→ Harvest	25	21	21	17	15	11	8	4/31	1/29	27	22	19
nion loured)	→ Sow (soil at 10 °C/50 °F*)		4/13	3/12/30	9/27				14/23	10/20			
	→ Thin, plant, hoe				17	15	11	8	4/31	1/29	27	22	
	→ Harvest					15	11	8	4/31	1/29			
nion hite)	→ Sow (soil at 10 °C/50 °F*)	8/17	4/13	3/12/30	9/27				14/23	10/20			
	→ Thin, plant, hoe			21	17	15	11	8		1/29	27	22	
	→ Harvest					15	11	8					
tato	→ Plant		21	21	17								
	→ Earth up, hoe, harvest				17	15	11	8	4/31	1/29			
dish	→ Sow (soil at 12 °C/53 °F*)	8/17	4/13	3/12/30	9/27	6/24	2/20/30	1/18/27	14/23	10/20	7/17	4/13	1/10/28
	→ Thin, harvest	25	21	21	17	15	11	8	4/31	1/29	27	22	19
lsify	→ Sow (soil at 15 °C/59 °F*)			3/12/30	9/27	6/24			14/23				
	→ Thin, hoe				17	15	11	8	4/31	1/29	27		
	→ Harvest	25	21								27	22	19
allot	→ Plant, weed	25	21	21	17	15	11	8			27	22	
	→ Harvest						11	8	4/31				
rnip	→ Sow (soil at 15 °C/59 °F*)	8/17	4/13	3/12/30	9/27	6/24	2/20/30	1/18/27	14/23				
	→ Thin, hoe, water		21	21	17	15	11	8	4/31	1/29	27		
	→ Harvest				17	15	11	8	4/31	1/29	27		

The cultivation of the vegetable is explained in the Calendar on the highlighted date.
*Ideal soil temperature for good germination.
** See more in leafy vegetables (p. 107).

Fruit vegetables

- Sow and plant in the greenhouse, under cover or in the open depending on the season and the climate of your garden
- Sow with the ascendant Moon in Aries ♈ or Sagittarius ♐
- Do all other work with the descending Moon in Leo ♌

	Jan	Feb	Mar	Apr	May	Jun	Jul	Aug	Sep	Oct	Nov	Dec
Aubergine												
→ Sow (in warm location at 20 °C/68 °F*)		2/12	1/11/28									
→ Transplant, plant, prune		20	18	15	12	9	6	3/29	26			
→ Harvest							26	13/22	9/18	6/16		
Beans												
→ Sow (soil at 10–12 °C/50–53 °F*)					5/23	1/19/28	26	13				
→ Hoe, earth up						9	6	3/29	26			
→ Harvest							26	13/22	9/18	6/16		
Broad beans (fava)												
→ Sow (soil at 8–10 °C/46–50 °F*)	6/16	2/12	1/11/28						6/16		2/12/30	9/27
→ Hoe, earth up, cut tops	23	20	18	15	12	9	6				19	17
→ Harvest				7/25	5/23	1/19/28	26	13/22				
Pepper (chilli and sweet)												
→ Sow (in warm location at 20 °C/68 °F*)		2/12	1/11/28									
→ Transplant, plant, cut back		20	18	15	12	9	6	3/29	26			
→ Harvest							26	13/22	9/18	6/16		
Cucumber												
→ Sow (soil at 18 °C/64 °F*)			1/11/28	7/25	5/23	1/19/28						
→ Thin, plant, prune			18	15	12	9	6	3/29	26			
→ Harvest						1/19/28	26	13/22	9/18	6/16		
Melon												
→ Sow (soil at 20 °C/68 °F*)			1/11/28	7/25	5/23							
→ Transplant, plant, cut back				15	12	9	6	3/29				
→ Harvest							26	13/22	9/18			
Peas												
→ Sow (soil at 10 °C/50 °F*)	6/16	2/12	1/11/28	7/25	5/23					6/16	2/12/30	9/27
→ Hoe, earth up	23	20		15	12	9	6				19	17
→ Harvest				7/25	5/23	1/19/28	26	13				
Marrow and courgette (zucchini)												
→ Sow (soil at 14 °C/57 °F*)			1/11/28	7/25	5/23	1/19/28	26					
→ Thin, plant, prune			18	15	12	9	6	3/29	26			
→ Harvest							26	13/22	9/18	6/16		
Strawberry												
→ Plant			18	15				3/29	26	23		
→ Harvest					5/23	1/19/28	26	13/22	9/18	6/16		
Tomato												
→ Sow (soil at 16–20 °C/60–68 °F*)			2/12	1/11/28								
→ Transplant, plant, prune				18	15	12	9	6	3/29	26		
→ Harvest							19/28	26	13/22	9/18	6/16	

The cultivation of the vegetable is explained in the Calendar on the highlighted date.

*Ideal soil temperature for good germination.

In the Orchard

- Plant, prune, clear and make cuttings with the descending Moon in Leo ♌
- Graft in the ascending Moon in Aries ♈ or Sagittarius ♐

		Jan	Feb	Mar	Apr	May	Jun	Jul	Aug	Sep	Oct	Nov	Dec
Fruit Trees and Shrubs													
Plant	→ Prepare planting holes, fertilise	23	20	18	15				29	26	23	19	17
	→ Plant fruit trees and soft-fruit shrubs	23	20	18	15					26	23	19	17
Prune	→ Crops with pips: apple, pear trees and grapes	23	20	18								19	17
	→ Apricot and peach trees		20	18									
	→ Soft-fruit bushes	23	20	18			9	6	3/29				
	→ When green, prune apples, pears, grapes						9	6	3/29				
	→ After the harvest, prune apricot and peach trees								3/29	26			
Treat trees	→ With white oil in winter	23	20									19	17
	→ With fungicide twice a year: before budding and when leaves fall		20	18							23	19	
Thin	→ Apples, pears, peaches					12	9						
Propagate	→ Make cuttings of soft-fruit shrubs	23	20	18								19	17
	→ Graft fruit-bearing trees			1/11/28	7/25		1/19/28	26	13/22				
	→ Layer grapes and kiwi			18	15	12	9						
Olive Trees													
	→ Plant			18									
	→ Prune, treat		20	18							23	19	
	→ Fertilise				15	12		6			23		

Wood for Timber and Heating

	Jan	Feb	Mar	Apr	May	Jun	Jul	Aug	Sep	Oct	Nov	Dec
Cut down large trees, cut up trunks, split logs	In descending Moon: January 1–5, January 20–February 1, February 17–28, March 16–27.									In descending Moon: October 1–4, October 21–November 1, November 17–28, December 14–25.		

The cultivation of the vegetable is explained in the Calendar on the highlighted date.

In the Ornamental Garden

- Thin, transplant, cut back, make cuttings, layer, divide and fertilise with the descending Moon in Gemini ♊ or Libra ♎
- Sow and graft with the ascending Moon in Aquarius ♒

Annual flowers

nasturtium, petunia, zinnia, clarkia...

	Jan	Feb	Mar	Apr	May	Jun	Jul	Aug	Sep	Oct	Nov	Dec
Sow	10	6	5	2/29	27	24		16	12	11		3/31
Thin, transplant, plant	1/20/28	16/24	16/24	12/20	18	6/14	3/11/31			1/21/29		

Biennial flowers

wallflower, forget-me-not, daisy, pansy...

	Jan	Feb	Mar	Apr	May	Jun	Jul	Aug	Sep	Oct	Nov	Dec
Sow					27	24	20	16				
Thin, transplant, plant						6/14	3/11/31	7/27		4/23	1/21/29	

Perennial flowers

oriental poppy, hollyhock, columbine, aster, peony...

	Jan	Feb	Mar	Apr	May	Jun	Jul	Aug	Sep	Oct	Nov	Dec
Sow			5		27	24	20	16	12	11	6	
Thin, transplant, plant				12/20		6/14	3/11/31	7/27	4/23	1/21/29	17	
Divide		16/24		12/20				7/27	4/23	1/21/29	17	

Perennial bulbs

Spring flowering

snowdrop, crocus, anemone, narcissus, hyacinth, tulip...

	Jan	Feb	Mar	Apr	May	Jun	Jul	Aug	Sep	Oct	Nov	Dec
Plant		16/24	16/24						4/23	1/21/29	17/25	
Divide		16/24	16/24		18	6/14						

Summer flowering

	Jan	Feb	Mar	Apr	May	Jun	Jul	Aug	Sep	Oct	Nov	Dec
madonna lily — Plant							31	7/27	4			
other lilies — Plant		16/24	16/24						4/23	1/21/29	17/25	
canna, dahlia, gladiola... — Plant	1/20/28	16/24	16/24	12/20	18							
canna, dahlia, gladiola... — Thin					18	6/14	3/11/31	7/27	4/23			
canna, dahlia, gladiola... — Pull out										1/21/29	17/25	

Perennial rhizomes

iris

	Jan	Feb	Mar	Apr	May	Jun	Jul	Aug	Sep	Oct	Nov	Dec
Plant, divide						6/14	3/11/31	7/27				

Perennial climbers

clematis, honeysuckle, wisteria...

	Jan	Feb	Mar	Apr	May	Jun	Jul	Aug	Sep	Oct	Nov	Dec
Plant	1/20/28	16/24	16/24	12/20					23	1/21/29	17/25	14/22
Prune		16/24	16/24								17/25	14/22
Layer				12/20	18	6/14	3/11/31	7/27				

Roses

	Jan	Feb	Mar	Apr	May	Jun	Jul	Aug	Sep	Oct	Nov	Dec
Plant	1/20/28	16/24	16/24								17/25	14/22
Prune suckers		16/24	16/24								17/25	
Remove dead leaves							3/11/31	7/27				
Deadhead flowers					18	6/14	3/11/31	7/27	4/23	1/21/29		
Take cuttings								7/27	4/23			
Fertilise		16/24	16/24								17/25	14/22
T-bud (shield graft)								16	12			

Spring or summer-blooming shrubs

magnolia, forsythia, lilac, rhododendron, hydrangea...

	Jan	Feb	Mar	Apr	May	Jun	Jul	Aug	Sep	Oct	Nov	Dec
Plant	1/20/28	16/24	16/24	12/20					23	1/21/29	17/25	14/22
Prune			16/24	12/20	18	6/14				1/21/29		
Take cuttings			16/24	12/20	18	6/14	3/11/31	7/27	4/23			
Fertilise		16/24	16/24								17/25	14/22
Graft		6	5			24	20	16	12			

The cultivation of the vegetable is explained in the Calendar on the highlighted date.

Trees, shrubs, leafy climbers and vines
- Plant, cut back, prune, cut stakes, clear and plant cuttings with the descending Moon in Cancer ♋ or Scorpio ♏.

		Jan	Feb	Mar	Apr	May	Jun	Jul	Aug	Sep	Oct	Nov	Dec
Conifers													
cedar, cypress, thuja, pine, fir, spruce…	Plant	3		17/26	13/22					6/24	3/22/30		
	Prune			17/26	13/22				1/9/28	6/24			
	Take cuttings								1/9/28	6/24			
Deciduous trees and shrubs													
birch, hornbeam, maple, beech, poplar, plane tree, prunus, willow…	Plant	3/30	18/26	17/26	13/22						3/22/30	18/27	15/24
	Prune		18/26	17/26	13/22		7/16	4/13/31	1/9/28	6/24			
	Thin	3/30	18/26									18/27	15/24
	Remove stakes	3/30	18/26									18/27	15/24
	Brush						7/16	4/13/31	1/9/28				
	Take cuttings		18/26	17/26			7/16	4/13/31	1/9/28	6/24	3/22/30	18/27	
Evergreen shrubs and bushes													
boxwood, spindle tree, holly, bay (laurel)…	Plant		18/26	17/26	13/22					6/24	3/22/30	18/27	
	Prune		18/26	17/26	13/22	11/20	7/16		1/9/28	6/24			
	Take cuttings		18/26	17/26					1/9/28	6/24			
Vines and climbers													
ivy, Virginia creeper…	Plant		18/26	17/26	13/22					6/24	3/22/30	18/27	15/24
	Prune			17/26		11/20	7/16	4/13/31	1/9/28				
	Take cuttings			17/26	13/22						3/22/30	18/27	

The lawn
- Sow with the ascending Moon in Pisces ♓
- Do all other tasks with the descending Moon in Cancer ♋ or Scorpio ♏.

		Jan	Feb	Mar	Apr	May	Jun	Jul	Aug	Sep	Oct	Nov	Dec
Bare spots	→ Rake the soil, spread mulch, roll				17/26	13/22	11/20		28	6			
	→ Sow, roll, water					4	2/29			15			
For new lawns	→ Prepare the soil			18/26	17/26	13/22			1/9/28	6			
	→ Spread compost			18/26	17/26	13/22			1/9/28	6			
	→ Level, rake, roll			18/26	17/26	13/22			1/9/28	6			
	→ Sow					4	2/29			15			
Yearly maintenance	→ Rake/scarify				17/26	13/22							
	→ Weed				17/26	13/22	11/20				6/24	3/22/30	
	→ Fertilise				17/26	13/22							15/24
	→ Mow, water				17/26	13/22	11/20	7/16	4/13/31	1/9/28	6/24	3/22/30	

In winter, don't walk on your lawn if it is frozen or under snow as you will damage the grass.

The cultivation of the vegetable is explained in the Calendar on the highlighted date.

Index

More books you might enjoy

Practical gardening advice

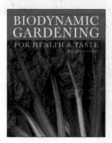

Explore the stars

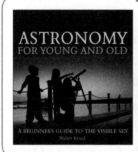

Nature activities with children

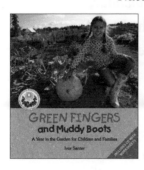

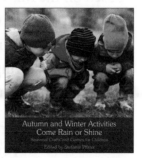

Why not try the
Maria Thun Biodynamic Calendar app?

Try it for free!

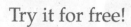 Automatically adjusts to your time-zone –
no need for manual calculations

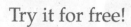 Ideal for farmers and gardeners worldwide

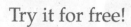 Choose your language – English, German or Dutch

Based on the *Maria Thun Biodynamic Calendar*,
the app is a quick, easy way to look up the key sowing
and planting information by date or type of action
(harvesting, sowing, grafting, etc) – and it's always in
your pocket on your phone.

For iPhone and iPad.